Improving Achievement With Digital Age Best Practices

Christopher M. Moersch

CORWIN
A SAGE Company

CORWIN
A SAGE Company

FOR INFORMATION:

Corwin

A SAGE Company

2455 Teller Road

Thousand Oaks, California 91320

(800) 233-9936

www.corwin.com

SAGE Publications Ltd.

1 Oliver's Yard

55 City Road

London EC1Y 1SP

United Kingdom

SAGE Publications India Pvt. Ltd.

B 1/I 1 Mohan Cooperative Industrial Area

Mathura Road, New Delhi 110 044

India

SAGE Publications Asia-Pacific Pte. Ltd.

3 Church Street

#10-04 Samsung Hub

Singapore 049483

Printed in the United States of America

Library of Congress Cataloging-in-Publication Data

A catalog record of this book is available from the Library of Congress.

ISBN: 978-1-4522-5550-7

This book is printed on acid-free paper.

SFI Certified Sourcing
www.sfiprogram.org
SFI-00453

Acquisitions Editor: Arnis Burvikovs

Associate Editor: Desirée A. Bartlett

Editorial Assistant: Ariel Price

Production Editor: Melanie Birdsall

Copy Editor: Karin Rathert

Typesetter: C&M Digitals (P) Ltd.

Proofreader: Theresa Kay

Indexer: Karen Wiley

Cover Designer: Anupama Krishnan

13 14 15 16 17 10 9 8 7 6 5 4 3 2 1

Improving Achievement With Digital Age Best Practices

Contents

Preface

We live in a results-now world. Seldom do we hear about a college football coach, school superintendent, or a business CEO maintaining his or her job tenure without demonstrating both immediate and measureable results impacting the bottom line. Imagine legendary figures, such as college men's basketball coach Mike Krzyzewski—who has coached four national championship teams—getting fired after posting losing records during two of his first 3 years at Duke University or IBM's CEO Louis Gerstner, who posted an average net profit of $5.8 billion from 1994 to 2002, losing his job after his first year as CEO for generating a modest end-of-year profit of $3 billion in 1994.

School systems nationwide are notorious for following a similar modus operandi. The craze to bolster test scores often forces districts to expend the majority of available funding as well as their collective focus to this single purpose at the detriment of other competing initiatives (e.g., 21st Century Skills, differentiated instruction, student-directed learning environments). Employing a one-size-fits-all mentality to increase student achievement may achieve limited short-term success, but its long-term ramifications often result in school systems, especially those within an urban setting, repeating a vicious cycle of continuous remediation.

Technology Use Practices

The heavy investment that schools spend nationally on digital tools and resources (e.g., laptops, interactive whiteboards, mobile devices) in the United States exceeds five billion dollars annually, yet seldom are technology solutions factored into any viable equation for improving student academic achievement. In fact, the pervasive use of digital tools in K–12 classrooms has not changed dramatically during the past two decades. According to data released from the national LoTi® (Levels of Teaching Innovation) survey in 2012, the predominant LoTi level nationally remains at a LoTi Level 2.

At a LoTi Level 2, the instructional focus emphasizes content understanding and supports mastery learning and direct instruction. Student learning focuses on lower levels of cognitive processing (e.g., Bloom levels—remembering, understanding, applying; Webb's levels—recall and reproduction, working with skills and concepts). Digital and/or environmental resources are used by students for extension activities, enrichment exercises, or information gathering assignments that reinforce lower cognitive skill development relating to the content under investigation.

Digital Age Best Practices

How can school systems leverage their available digital tools and resources, curriculum initiatives, and limited local, state, and federal funding to achieve academic success in their schools? There is no single variable responsible for any school system's turnaround. Achieving success on all fronts of the curriculum and instruction spectrum requires a synergistic effort to maintain a high degree of fidelity to a common set of principles over the course of a lengthy period of time. These common principles are what I refer to as Digital Age Best Practices. These best practices include

- **Bolstering purposeful inquiry through student questions**
- **Promoting shared expertise with networked collaboration**
- **Personalizing and globalizing content by making authentic connections**
- **Accelerating individual growth through vertical and horizontal differentiation**
- **Anchoring student learning with digital age tools and resources**
- **Clarifying student understanding with formative assessments**
- **Implementing student-centered learning environments**

The term *digital age* is used judiciously to signify a set of classroom best practices that (a) can be seamlessly expanded when used in conjunction with digital tools and resources (e.g., mobile devices, interactive whiteboards, digital responders) and/or (b) apply the principles of 21st Century Skills (e.g., critical thinking and problem solving, communication and collaboration).

The use of the Digital Age Best Practices provides a solid foundation for instructional decision making while supporting other district initiatives, such as new teacher evaluation systems, classroom walkthrough protocols, academic benchmarking, differentiated instruction, technology integration, and "conventional" best practices in the classroom.

Can school systems designated as low achieving according to state and federal guidelines achieve academic excellence? Exemplars do exist that document the efficacy of Digital Age Best Practices, strategic team building, flexible professional development, and shared accountability to bring forth such dramatic improvement. One example is the Atlantic City School District in Atlantic City, New Jersey. This urban school system comprised of a 98% Title 1 population in the PreK–8 schools was designated as a high performing district by the New Jersey Department of Education during the 2011 through 2012 school year—one of a handful of urban school systems in the state to move from a "school in need of improvement" to "high performing."

A Different Approach

This book chronicles how one urban school district, Atlantic City Public Schools, overcame institutional inertia, poverty, and gang violence to elevate student and teacher performance with dwindling federal and state financial resources through a common set of best practices known as Digital Age Best Practices. These best practices, however, are not limited to an urban setting but flourish equally well within any K–12 school system. Collectively, they can help transform static, didactic bastions of information processing into vibrant learning communities without the need for additional spending. The Digital Age Best Practices can provide value-added benefits to schools that have already invested heavily in well-conceived initiatives ranging from *one-to-x* mobile device acquisitions to a new math adoption.

The organization of this manuscript uses the common thread of the Atlantic City Public Schools as the backdrop to highlight both success stories as well as the obvious challenges embedded with implementing the change cycle. To this end, the book is divided into four progressive stages. Section I discusses each of the seven Digital Age Best Practices, including implementation challenges and their corresponding solutions, while Section II offers a broader perspective of Digital Age Best Practices within the context of national, state, and local initiatives. Section III provides a specific road map that school systems can follow to retrofit the Digital Age Best Practices into their own unique teaching and learning paradigm. Section IV highlights specific characteristics required of instructional leaders in the 21st century to optimize the benefits of Digital Age Best Practices, resulting in increased student academic progress and improved classroom pedagogy.

A Word of Caution

The reader, however, should not be confused by the book's sequential organization. The book is far from being a "how-to" instructional manual; rather, it is a guide to both tantalize and inform the reader with suggestions, illustrations, examples, and strategies aimed at elevating the teaching and learning experience. The use of well-intentioned theories is kept to a minimum; instead, the book relies on pragmatic examples that have helped many classroom teachers engage seemingly disgruntled, disenfranchised learners. The enclosed collection of sample lesson plans, frameworks, implementation strategies, and truisms is best utilized by readers who

- desire suggestions based on actual experiences rather than on theoretical constructs,
- recognize that change can be a slow yet satisfying process, and
- are willing to do the work.

Yet, a word of caution is offered as you peruse the ensuring sections. *Don't be concerned about making too many changes too fast!* To paraphrase Dr. Robert Marzano from his speech to the New Jersey Federal Providers Association in 2012, even incremental change in teacher effectiveness can have a statistically significant impact on student achievement.

Acknowledgments

I would like to express my heartfelt gratitude to the many individuals who saw me through this adventure; to all those who provided encouragement, talked things over, read, wrote, offered comments, allowed me to quote their remarks and, in some instances, borrow their ideas.

I am deeply indebted to the work of our LoTi Team, LeeChel, Dennee, Fred, Mark, and Jeremiah, who provided the foundation for this work. I want to especially thank LeeChel Moersch, my wife, partner, and co-collaborator, who provided the initial idea for writing the book and who encouraged me through challenges too many to mention and orchestrated a clear pathway for the book's completion. I would like to thank representatives of the Atlantic City Board of Education and especially Marilyn Cohen, who provided the inspiration and insight into the operation of a high-performing urban school system.

Publisher's Acknowledgments

Corwin gratefully acknowledges the contributions of the following reviewers:

Roxie R. Ahlbrecht, Teacher, Consultant, Adjunct Faculty
Sioux Falls Public Schools, Augustana College
Sioux Falls, SD

Neil MacNeill, Head Master
Ellenbrook Independent Primary School
Ellenbrook, Western Australia, Australia

Leslie Standerfer, Principal
Estrella Foothills High School
Goodyear, AZ

Kathy Tritz-Rhodes, Principal
Marcus-Meriden-Cleghorn Schools
Marcus, IA

Bonnie Tryon, Former President
School Administrators Association of New York State (SAANYS)
Latham, NY

About the Author

 For the past fifteen years, **Dr. Christopher M. Moersch** has been the principal investigator of the LoTi project and Executive Director of LoTi Connection Inc. In that capacity, he has worked with thousands of educators nationwide promoting the tenets of digital age literacy and professional development in an effort to transform low performing schools into high performing schools. He has more than twenty years' experience in the areas of curriculum development, program evaluation, and technology integration practices. His specialization includes implementing school improvement initiatives, creating 21st century learning environments, and facilitating organizational change.

Introduction

Efforts to achieve pervasive digital age learning in our urban schools have often been thwarted by perceived competing initiatives ranging from conventional school reform efforts (e.g., Direct Instruction, Success for All) to popular curriculum models (Understanding by Design, Learning-Focused Solutions, Universal Design for Learning)—all with the hope of improving instruction and student achievement on high-stakes tests. Fortunately, powerful exemplars do exist that demonstrate digital age learning's potential for rigorous and relevant learning experiences that target specific core content areas in math, language arts literacy, social studies, and science. One need look no further than popular educational websites, including the George Lucas Educational Foundation (www.edutopia.org), ePals (www.epals.org), and eCybermission (www.ecybermission.com) for compelling proof of digital age learning's efficacy to promote high levels of student engagement, collaborative learning, and authentic problem solving.

What makes these digital age exemplars so engaging to students? More importantly, what impact do Digital Age Best Practices have on student academic growth in the classroom? In the current era of high-stakes testing, building and district stakeholders are looking for proven, research-based methods that have demonstrably been shown to impact student achievement. In 2001, Marzano, Pickering, and Pollock identified nine research-based instructional strategies that when implemented "correctly" produced a reported statistically significant effect size on student achievement based on standardized test measures (see Figure A).

Though these instructional strategies have been employed at varying degrees by school systems nationwide to improve student academic achievement, their collective impact on transitioning

Figure A   Research-Based Best Practices

1. Comparing, contrasting, classifying, analogies, and metaphors (effect size = 1.61 or 45 percentile points)

2. Summarizing and note taking (effect size = 1.0 or 34 percentile points)

3. Reinforcing effort and giving praise (effect size = 0.8 or 29 percentile points)

4. Homework and practice (effect size = 0.77 or 28 percentile points)

5. Nonlinguistic representation (effect size = 0.75 or 27 percentile points)

6. Cooperative learning (effect size = 0.74 or 27 percentile points)

7. Setting objectives and providing feedback (effect size = 0.61 or 23 percentile points)

8. Generating and testing hypotheses (effect size = 0.61 or 23 percentile points)

9. Cues, questions, and advanced organizers (effect size = 0.59 or 22 percentile points)

Source: Marzano et al. (2001)

traditional classroom pedagogy from subject-matter-based learning to digital age learning has been minimal. Besides Marzano et al. (2001), the research community has articulated additional variables impacting student achievement, including direct teaching, advanced organizers, meta-cognition, and mastery learning, yet none have directly altered conventional classroom roles and routines.

How do school systems such as the Atlantic City Public Schools maximize their available personnel, equipment, and instructional resources to achieve unprecedented levels of student academic growth? Is there a universal set of instructional strategies that can (a) serve as a catalyst to promote digital age learning in the schools, (b) support existing district initiatives relating to literacy and math achievement, and (c) provide empirical support for improving test scores. Research has documented a common set of strategies known as Digital Age Best Practices that when applied and used in conjunction with the aforementioned instructional strategies can elevate student academic growth beyond those documented by conventional best practices alone.

The overall increase in student achievement in the Atlantic City School District mirrored improvements in other areas, including a marked increase in high school graduation rates, greater student matriculation to top-flight universities, an elevated percentage of honor students, a higher quality of instruction, and improved school climate systemwide. The high school graduation rate increased from 92% in 2006 to 98% in 2011. The percentage of top twenty students in the Class of 2011 from the minority-fed Atlantic City area increased from 0% in 2006 to 65% in 2011. Qualitative data tracking school climate, teacher efficacy, and student empowerment revealed that the vast majority of teachers, supervisors, and building administrators concurred with the current direction of the district in terms of instructional improvement.

Classroom walkthrough data at all Atlantic City School District campuses revealed similar changes in classroom pedagogy and student learning. Based on classroom walkthrough data (see Figure B), the level of student cognition in the classroom increased districtwide from a mean score of 3.23 during the 2007 through 2008 school year, representing the Understanding level of Bloom's Taxonomy, to a mean score of 3.92, representing the Applying level of Bloom's Taxonomy, during the 2011 through 2012 school year.

Similar findings were noted for engaged learning, where 2007 through 2008 walkthroughs revealed that the mean level of Engagement increased from 2.57 (students collaborating to report what they have learned with possible options) to a mean Engagement level of 3.34 (students solving teacher-directed problems) during the 2011 through 2012 school year. Students' ability to make real-world connections to the content increased significantly from a mean 3.41 (students making limited real-world connections) in 2007 through 2008 to a mean Authentic Connections level of 3.86 (students making extensive real-world connections) during the 2011 through 2012 school year.

Has an urban school system, such as Atlantic City School District, achieved all of its goals based on a single battery of state assessments? The answer is no. Student achievement scores both on criterion-referenced and norm-reference indicators need to show continued growth. The quality of teaching needs to move to higher levels of student engagement resulting in behaviors consistent with a student-directed learning environment. The level of student cognition also needs to advance to a routine level at the higher Bloom levels (i.e., analyzing, evaluating, creating). Nonachievement data relating to school climate, student and teacher satisfaction, and community support similarly need to show continuous improvement.

Figure B   Atlantic City Schools Walkthrough Data

Category	2007–08	2011–12	Difference	Statistically Significant
Higher-Order Thinking	3.23	3.92	0.69	Yes $P = 0.0001$
Engage Learning	2.57	3.34	0.77	Yes $P = 0.0001$
Authentic Connections	3.41	3.86	0.45	Yes $P = 0012$
Technology Use	2.94	2.88	0.06	No

Yet, the critical attributes of many of the Digital Age Best Practices addressing collaborative problem solving, differentiated instruction, technology integration, and formative assessment practices have established a firm foothold within the collective mindset of the Atlantic City Public School's K–12 learning community. The pervasive use of these best practices at the operational level is what gives hope to continued improvements in both qualitative and quantitative indicators in the years ahead.

SECTION I

Digital Age Best Practices

D igital Age Best Practices represent a distinct set of instructional
strategies that contain empirically validated results relating to
student academic achievement while promoting the tenets of digital
age learning. Each Digital Age Best Practice was selected based on the
following criteria:

- Aligns to the National Educational Technology Standards for
  Students (NETS-S) and 21st Century Skills
- Demonstrates significant results on standardized tests
- Employs existing classroom digital tools and resources
- Provides results that can be generalized to any K–12 classroom
- Allows seamless integration with other "competing" instruc-
  tional initiatives

The Digital Age Best Practices provide classroom practitioners
with a balanced approach to addressing instructional practices that
have demonstrated "statistical significance," but of equal importance,
have promoted the critical attributes of 21st Century Skills and
Themes. A summary of each Digital Age Best Practice follows.

Digital Age Best Practice 1: Bolstering Purposeful Inquiry Through Student Questions

Critical Look-Fors

- Student-generated questions drive the inquiry
- Evidence of one or more teacher-generated focus activities
- Presence of complex thinking processes
- Presence of a student-directed learning environment

Student-directed inquiry represents the process of students guiding their own inquiry through self-generated questions based on the dissonance created between the student and his or her psychological, physical, or digital environment. Creating this dissonance is often a result of the student's exposure to and interaction with an event, a self-generated problem or challenge, or a critical observation. Teachers seeking to promote inquiry often capitalize on some type of focus activity (e.g., staged scenarios, discrepant events, world events, word clouds, engaging video clips) that enables students to connect to the content in an authentic manner and generate purposeful questions about the topic.

Contemporary instructional models including the Universal Design for Learning (UDL), 5E Model (Bybee et al., 2006), Experiential-Based Action Model (Moersch,1994), problem-based learning, and issues-based science capitalize on this approach, providing the classroom teacher with a set of guidelines to transform didactic learning environments into purposeful centers of student inquiry. According to the National Science Education Standards (1996), "When engaging in inquiry, students describe objects and events, ask questions, construct explanations, test those explanations against current scientific knowledge, and communicate their ideas to others. They identify their assumptions, use critical and logical thinking, and consider alternative explanations" (p. 13).

Current meta-analytical research findings confirm positive gains on student academic achievement when comparing student-centered inquiry to conventional instruction (Preston, 2008; Schroeder et al., 2007). Independent studies by Anderson (2002) and Kessner (2008) documented similar findings. In research studies that address the usefulness of *project-based learning*, an instructional methodology grounded in student inquiry and authentic problem solving, Geier et al. (2008) and Mergendoller, Maxwell, and Bellisimo (2007) demonstrated that project-based learning was more effective than traditional instruction in increasing academic achievement on annual state-administered assessment tests as well as teaching specific content areas, such as science and economics.

The evidence suggests that the role of student inquiry using a student-centered learning model has strong merit as a Digital Age Best Practice. As with any best practice, whether digitally based or conventional, the fidelity of implementation ultimately determines the magnitude of the effect on student achievement.

Digital Age Best Practice 2: Promoting Shared Expertise With Networked Collaboration

Structured social networking, a cornerstone of digital age learning, is not to be confused with students randomly accessing and updating their Twitter or Facebook account. As a Digital Age Best Practice, structured networked collaboration supports the concept of connectivism, whereby learning is viewed as a process of creating connections among information sources and developing networks. A network, in this context, may be a community of learners (e.g., a classroom), a digital environment, or a social structure where ideas are shared with others, thereby "cross-pollinating" the learning environment (Siemens, 2005).

Critical Look-Fors

- Students able to articulate a common group goal
- Evidence of student problem solving and/or issues resolution
- Individual and group accountability structures in place
- Employment of digital tools and resources (e.g., blogs, wikis, online threaded discussion forums) to promote collaboration

When defining networked collaboration, a distinction needs to be made between cooperative and collaborative learning. Though both cooperative and collaborative learning involve students working in groups toward the completion of a task as well as sharing and comparing procedures and conclusions, cooperative learning tends to be more teacher centered than collaborative learning. Collaborative learning involves the empowerment of students for the purpose of finding solutions to problems and making inferences and drawing conclusions even though they may be different from the teacher's perspective.

The positive impact of cooperative learning on student academic achievement is well documented in the research literature (Dotson,

2001; Johnson & Johnson, 1999; Slavin, 1991). According to Slavin (1995), "Cooperative learning has its greatest effects on student learning when groups are recognized or rewarded based on individual learning of their members. Research has found greater achievement gains for cooperative methods using group goals and individual accountability than for those that do not" (p. 41). In a meta-analysis investigating the impact of teaching strategies on science achievement scores, the presence of a collaborative learning environment was cited as significant in terms of its link to improved student achievement (Schroeder et al., 2007).

As a Digital Age Best Practice, collaborative learning involves student participation in a learning community for the purpose of clarifying, assimilating, or generating new concepts or ideas. Collaborative learning retains the benefits of the cooperative learning structure but promotes higher-order thinking processes, purposeful problem solving and decision making, and issues resolution. The impact of structured collaborative networking on student academic achievement is less documented than cooperative learning given the relative infancy of this instructional approach. Baker, Gearhart, and Herman (1994) found that technology-enriched collaborative learning environments seem to result in new experiences for students that require higher-level reasoning and problem solving—two variables often linked to improved student achievement.

Studies conducted by Wade (1994) and Teele (2006) reported similar findings involving groups of elementary and middle school students, respectively. Students exposed to a collaborative learning environment achieved higher posttest scores in literacy and mathematics when compared to their control group counterparts. Although the available research on networked collaboration is modest compared to cooperative learning, we considered its potential in light of the empirical data supporting group learning configurations in general.

Digital Age Best Practice 3: Personalizing and Globalizing Content by Making Authentic Connections

Authentic contextual bridges provide the foundation for students to connect what they are learning in class to the real world. Herrington, Oliver, and Reeves (2002) identified ten characteristics of authentic learning that can be adapted to any subject area (Figure C).

As a Digital Age Best Practice, creating authentic contextual bridges can be accomplished by integrating one or more 21st Century Themes as articulated by the Partnership for the 21st Century (2013). These themes include global awareness; financial, economic, business entrepreneurial literacy; civic literacy; health literacy; and environmental literacy. Encasing these themes within a well-conceived and standards-aligned performance task can elevate the rigor and relevance associated with any content area.

Critical Look-Fors

- Learning connected to one or more 21st Century Themes
- Outcomes require sustained investigation
- Emphasis on multiple interpretations and outcomes
- Learning possesses an interdisciplinary perspective

Figure C   Ten Characteristics of Authentic Learning

1. **Real-World Relevance.** Authentic activities match the real-world tasks of professionals in practice as nearly as possible. Learning rises to the level of authenticity when it asks students to work actively with abstract concepts, facts, and formulae inside a realistic—and highly social—context mimicking "the ordinary practices of the [disciplinary] culture."

2. **Ill-Defined Problem.** Challenges cannot be solved easily by the application of an existing algorithm; instead, authentic activities are relatively undefined and open to multiple interpretations, requiring students to identify for themselves the tasks and subtasks needed to complete the major task.

3. **Sustained Investigation.** Problems cannot be solved in a matter of minutes or even hours. Instead, authentic activities comprise complex tasks to be investigated by students over a sustained period of time, requiring significant investment of time and intellectual resources.

4. **Multiple Sources and Perspectives.** Learners are not given a list of resources. Authentic activities provide the opportunity for students to examine the task from a variety of theoretical and practical perspectives, using a variety of resources, and requires students to distinguish relevant from irrelevant information in the process.

5. **Collaboration.** Success is not achievable by an individual learner working alone. Authentic activities make collaboration integral to the task, both within the course and in the real world.

(Continued)

Figure C (Continued)

6. **Reflection (Metacognition).** Authentic activities enable learners to make choices and reflect on their learning, both individually and as a team or community.

7. **Interdisciplinary Perspective.** Relevance is not confined to a single domain or subject matter specialization. Instead, authentic activities have consequences that extend beyond a particular discipline, encouraging students to adopt diverse roles and think in interdisciplinary terms.

8. **Integrated Assessment.** Assessment is not merely summative in authentic activities but is woven seamlessly into the major task in a manner that reflects real-world evaluation processes.

9. **Polished Products.** Conclusions are not merely exercises or substeps in preparation for something else. Authentic activities culminate in the creation of a whole product, valuable in its own right.

10. **Multiple Interpretations and Outcomes.** Rather than yielding a single correct answer obtained by the application of rules and procedures, authentic activities allow for diverse interpretations and competing solutions.

Source: Herrington, Oliver, and Reeves (2003)

A clear delineation needs to be made between authentic performance tasks and authentic assessments. Authentic performance tasks become authentic assessments when scoring criteria is developed and shared with students. The goal is for students to internalize the criteria, establish milestones, and be able to monitor their own progress. According to Mueller (2005), "Authentic assessment is a form of assessment in which students are asked to perform real-world tasks that demonstrate meaningful application of essential knowledge and skills" (p. 2).

Research on various forms of authentic learning, such as students making authentic connections and integrated-curriculum programs, lend support to its inclusion as a Digital Age Best Practice. In a meta-analysis conducted by Hartzler (2000), "students in integrated curricular programs consistently out-performed students in traditional classes on national standardized tests, on statewide testing programs, and on program-developed assessment." Meissner (1999, Conclusion) investigated the impact of problem-posing instruction on mathematical problem solving among seventh-grade students and found a statistically significant difference between those students who received some type of problem-posing instruction and those who did not. Problem-posing instruction employs authentic, personally meaningful learning experiences as the basis for students to make sense out of their world by building connections between previous and new knowledge.

Though research provides empirical support for both *making authentic connections* and *student-directed inquiry* as separate Digital Age Best Practices, their combined effect in the classroom can provide the foundation for even more powerful learning.

Digital Age Best Practice 4: Accelerating Individual Growth Through Vertical and Horizontal Differentiation

In a differentiated classroom, the content, process, and product of learning are adjusted based on the readiness level, interests, and learning profile of the students. In a differentiated learning environment, the teacher

- addresses student differences both horizontally and vertically,
- adjusts the elements of the curriculum to match student needs,
- ensures that students participate in respectful work, and
- collaborates with students in the learning process.

Critical Look-Fors

- Adjustments to the content, process, and/or product based on learner readiness, profile, and interests are documented
- Presence of learning centers/ stations
- Digital tools and resources adjusted to the needs of the learner
- Multiple LoTi levels simultaneously employed in the classroom

An abundance of research findings (Kegerise, 2007; Luster, 2008; Slemmer, 2002) have found positive links between differentiated instruction and student achievement. Its inclusion as a Digital Age Best Practice has more to do with the complexity and diversity of students entering classrooms across the United States than with its alignment to the characteristics of the "defined" digital age learner (e.g., digital native). How do you promote the tenets of differentiation in school settings with multiple dominant languages, a large variance in socioeconomic levels, and distinct cultural differences? Here lies the challenge.

In a digital age differentiated classroom, the existing digital resources are used strategically by the teacher to adjust instruction either horizontally (e.g., student interests, learning modalities) or vertically (e.g., student reading levels). Instruction is delivered at multiple LoTi (Levels of Teaching Innovation) levels based on individual student or group learning profiles. LoTi is a framework conceptualized by Moersch (1995) that describes different levels of teaching practices with graduated levels of authenticity, complex thinking, student-centeredness, and technology use as one moves from a lower to a higher level of teaching innovation.

Accommodating the needs of today's digital natives requires multiple skill sets. The educator must be well versed in both specific strategies to differentiate instruction (e.g., tiered instruction, personal agendas, anchor activities, learning contracts, compacted curriculum, flexible grouping) and the available digital tools and resources that promote differentiation (e.g., wikis, blogs, interactive applets, simulations).

Digital Age Best Practice 5: Anchoring Student Learning With Digital Age Tools and Resources

Critical Look-Fors

- Emphasis on content and process skills; not the digital tools
- Digital tools used at a LoTi 3 and higher
- Digital tools used in conjunction with clear, measureable achievement goals
- Use of digital tools is purposeful and intentional

For years, the term digital age tools and resources or its earlier alias, technology, have been the standard-bearer for 21st Century Skills. Yet, used in isolation, its effects on student achievement have been criticized (Wenglinsky, 1998). As noted by Papanastasiou, Zemblyas, and Vrasidas (2003), "It is not computer use itself that has a positive or negative effect on the science achievement of students, but the way in which computers are used" (p. 325). According to Perez-Prado and Thirunarayanan (2002) and Moersch (2009), higher student achievement gains were found in classrooms using technology in conjunction with inquiry-based teaching that emphasized collaborative learning methods, critical thinking, and problem-solving skills.

Roschelle, Pea, Hoadley, Gordin, and Means (2000) noted that technology can enhance both what and how children learn when used in conjunction with (1) active engagement, (2) participation in groups, (3) frequent interaction and feedback, and (4) connections to real-world contexts. Results of more than seven hundred empirical research studies, a statewide study, a national sample of fourth and eighth graders, and analysis of newer educational technologies demonstrate that students show positive gains in achievement on researcher-constructed instruments, national tests, and standardized tests when they participate in

- computer-assisted instruction,
- integrated learning systems technology,
- simulations that teach higher-order thinking,
- collaborative networked technologies, or
- design and programming technologies (Schacter, 1999).

These findings corroborate a meta-analysis conducted by Sandy-Hanson (2006) that indicated that students who are taught with technology outperform their peers who are taught with traditional methods of instruction. These findings also suggest digital age tool use is most telling when implemented in conjunction with the other Digital Age Best Practices. In the LoTi (Levels of Teaching Innovation) framework, the occurrence of digital tool use with complex thinking strategies (investigation, decision making) and collaborative problem solving is first encountered at a LoTi 3 (Figure 8.0).

As Archer (1998) reminds us, "What matters most are not the machines and the wiring themselves, but what teachers and students do with them . . . a constructivist approach toward learning, in which students work in rich environments of information and experience, often in groups, and build their own understandings about them—taps into the computer's greatest strengths" (p. 12).

Digital Age Best Practice 6: Clarifying Student Understanding With Formative Assessments

Formative assessments refer to both informal and formal activities used by teachers and students to provide information about individual and group academic progress for the purpose of adjusting or modifying instruction. Research supports the use of formative assessments as a viable strategy to improve student achievement (Black & Wiliam, 1998b; Fuch & Fuch, 1986; Wininger, 2005).

According to Black and Wiliam (1998a), "such assessment becomes formative when the evidence is actually used to adapt the teaching

Critical Look-Fors

- Follow-up interventions are timely, targeted, and based on student data
- Adequate wait time given for student responses
- Framed questions apply directly to content understanding
- Digital tools and resources (e.g., blogs, wikis, discussion forums) used for student feedback

work to meet the needs" (p. 2). Formal assessments provide more structure and greater reliability (e.g., common assessments, benchmark tests, performance tasks); informal assessments require less structure but are more frequent, transparent, and in many cases, student centered (e.g., teacher observations, minute papers, peer reviews, questions and answers, self-reflection, student journals, pair shares).

The inclusion of formative assessments as a Digital Age Best Practice is based on the reflective nature of the formative assessment process to promote personal progress. Shepard (2000) links formative or classroom assessment with the constructivist movement, which suggests that learning is an active process, building on previous knowledge, experience, skills, and interests.

The critical attributes of the formative assessment process are also linked to specific 21st Century Skills that address the importance of being flexible, adapting to change, and becoming self-directed learners; for example, incorporate feedback effectively; deal positively with praise, setbacks, and criticism; demonstrate commitment to learning as a lifelong process; and reflect critically on past experiences in order to inform future progress (Partnership for 21st Century Skills, 2011). According to Stiggins and Chappuis (2008), "It is the practice of assessment for learning that wields the proven power to help a whole new generation of students take responsibility for their own learning, become lifelong learners, and achieve at much higher levels" ("Taking Responsibility," para. 1).

Digital Age Best Practice 7: Implementing Student-Centered Learning Environments

In a student-directed learning environment, students are vested with more options and input into the teaching/learning dynamic than its conventional instructional counterpart, teacher-centered instruction. Gibbs (1992) describes student-centered learning as giving "students greater autonomy and control over choice of subject matter, learning methods, and pace of study" (p. 23) to make decisions governing their own learning.

The easiest way to think about student-centered learning is to visualize any learning experience as being divided into three components: content, process, and product. Content represents what students need to know or do; the process represents how the students will learn the content; and lastly, the product represents what the student(s) will

Critical Look-Fors

- Students talk exceeds teacher talk
- Emphasis on individual or small group learning
- Teacher/student negotiate learning opportunities
- Use of varied instructional materials/strategies

need to produce to demonstrate their mastery of the content. In a student-centered learning environment, students are given options, input, or control into one or more of these components.

Consider the content/process/product wheel within a student-centered learning environment addressing the causes of the American Revolutionary War. In this scenario, students are given opportunity to provide input, make choices, or control the overall focus of their own learning. For example, students may be presented with choices relating to the content (e.g., investigate the economic issues impacting the U.S. colonies or the political discontent with autocratic rule), process (e.g., participate in learning stations, use an options list, participate in an I-Search investigation, negotiate a learning contract), and/or product (e.g., submit a blog entry, conduct a formal presentation, prepare a voice thread, submit a peer-reviewed article).

In K–12 classrooms, the concept of student-centered learning may also appear in the guise of problem-based or project-based learning. Both are derivatives of a constructivist learning model that emphasizes guided student engagement in discovery learning. Each seeks to present students with a complex problem or challenge requiring student identification of and engagement in the knowledge and skills necessary to successfully solve the problem or address the challenge (Laitsch, 2007).

Problem-based learning represents students actively engaged in a purposeful investigation surrounding an ill-structured problem. According to Barrows (2002), the use of ill-structured problems prompts students to "generate not just multiple thoughts about the causes of the problem, but multiple thoughts on how to solve it" (pp. 119–122). Thomas (2000) identifies five criteria for defining problem-based learning. Problem-based learning

- is central and not peripheral to the curriculum,
- focuses on questions or problems that "drive" students to encounter (and struggle with) the central concepts and principals of the discipline,

- involves students in a constructive investigation,
- is student driven to some significant degree, and
- represents realistic, not school-like scenarios.

Research indicates that problem-based learning benefits students by increasing their motivation and engagement for a topic, and it produces a positive effect on student content knowledge and the development of collaborative, critical thinking, and problem solving skills (Center of Excellence in Leadership of Learning, 2009).

The impact of a student-centered learning environment on student achievement is well established. Research shows that providing students with choices in learning activities increases students' achievement, engagement, perceived competence, and levels of aspiration (Cordova & Lepper, 1996; Westberg & Archambault, 2004). Current meta-analytical study findings confirm positive gains on student academic achievement when comparing student-centered inquiry to conventional instruction (Smith, 1996). As reported earlier, Geier et al. (2008) and Mergendoller et al. (2007) demonstrated that PBL was more effective than traditional instruction in increasing academic achievement on annual state-administered assessment tests, and it teaches specific content areas, such as science and economics.

Meta-analyses conducted by Dochy et al. (2003) and Walker and Leary (2009) found a positive effect from PBL on the skills of students. In a study on the effects of learner-centered classrooms, Salinas and Garr (2009) found "that minorities in schools and classrooms with higher learner-centered orientations not only have test scores statistically equal of those from their white peers, but also that students in learner-centered environments have higher scores in the non-traditional measures, including tolerance and openness to diversity" (pp. 226–237).

The evidence suggests that the role of student inquiry using a student-centered learning model has strong merit as a Digital Age Best Practice. As mentioned earlier, the fidelity of implementation involving any best practice, whether digitally based or conventional, will ultimately determine the magnitude of its effect on student achievement.

The majority of the Digital Age Best Practices have demonstrated moderate to significant results relating to student academic achievement. These include clarifying student understanding with formative assessments (providing formative assessments), bolstering purposeful inquiry through student questions (self-questioning by students), promoting shared expertise with networked collaboration (cooperative versus individualistic learning), accelerating individual growth through vertical/horizontal differentiation (tactile stimulation programs), and implementing student-centered learning environments (student-centered teaching) (Wiggins, 2012).

Many, if not all, of the Digital Age Best Practices can be integrated seamlessly into any learning experience or curriculum initiative ranging from a single day lesson plan to a new reading program. As with other "research-based best practices," their combined impact on student achievement consistently produces the greatest overall effect size on student achievement. The same is true with the aforementioned Digital Age Best Practices. Their deliberate use in the instructional planning process in isolation, collectively, or in concert with other best practices provides students the best opportunity to maximize their academic success and prepare for their eventual matriculation into a digitally based global environment.

Chapters 1 through 7 will explore each of the Digital Age Best Practices in greater detail, with emphasis on practical application to the classroom. The ensuing chapters will discuss the implementation challenges facing each Digital Age Best Practices' integration into the urban school setting defined by the Atlantic City Board of Education experience. The reader will hopefully note the pivotal role of district level leadership in finding viable solutions to potential implementation barriers stemming from various stakeholders (e.g., teachers, parents, community members). Many of these barriers were overcome by an administrative team that possessed the *courage* to stay the course in light of quick-fix options, a *creative* spark to finding solutions, a *cultivating* mentality to empowering others, a *communication* acumen that embraced community members, staff, and students, and lastly, a deep-seated *commitment* to purposeful and thoughtful change.

with the look-fors of the Digital Age Best Practice *Bolstering purposeful inquiry through student questions.*

The 5E Learning Cycle is a method of structuring classroom lessons that are based upon constructivist learning theory, research-based best practices in reading pedagogy, and cognitive psychology. The model represents a recursive cycle of distinctive cognitive stages of learning that include Engage, Explore, Explain, Extend, and Evaluate. The flexibility of the 5E Model enables classroom teachers to complete a 5E lesson in a single class period (i.e., one day) or extend a particular lesson over several days, depending on the depth and breadth of the content as well as learner readiness. Provided below is an explanation of the 5E Model within the context of a middle school math lesson. The culminating task of the math lesson is for students to determine which animal in the animal kingdom is "most athletic" based on their application of fractions and ratio.

Engage

The first stage in the 5E Model is *Engage.* Engagement provides the necessary hook to sustain students in the learning to follow. Engagement activities might include a demonstration, a discussion, a simulation, or even a discrepant event that taps into prior knowledge about the content and engages the student's natural curiosity. These activities serve to uncover what students know and think about the content and its connections to the lesson's culminating performance task. It also prompts students to generate their own questions relating to the content as well as formulate a problem definition associated with the content under investigation.

Sample Math Lesson: Engagement Activities

- Students watch the video, *YouTube—Best Dunker*, as a *discrepant event* to view an athlete dunking a basketball at 5 ft. 10 in. but with a 56 in. vertical leap.
- Students generate a mean or average for a sixth-grade student's height, jumping ability, and leaping ability based on central tendency data generated from five volunteer students jumping (vertical leap) and leaping (standing broad jump) from a stationary position. This *demonstration* connects students' prior knowledge about central tendency (i.e., mean) to the task of determining the most "athletic" animal.

- Students watch the video, *YouTube–Deadly San Francisco Zoo Tiger Attack,* as another discrepant event to get them thinking about the athletic ability of different animals.
- Students compare their leaping and jumping ability to the leaping and jumping ability

Critical Look-Fors

- Creates interest
- Generates curiosity
- Raises questions
- Elicits responses that uncover what students know or think about the content

of a Siberian tiger as a ratio to promote their natural curiosity and provide a connection between the content (i.e., fractions and ratio) and themselves.

Explore

The second stage is *Explore.* Exploration enables students to manipulate concepts and ideas as they observe, question, and investigate the concepts to develop fundamental awareness of the nature of the materials and ideas. Students are encouraged to work together without direct instruction from the teacher.

Sample Math Lesson: Exploration Activities

- Students work in pairs to determine the strongest animal, based on its body weight, by creating a ratio of how much weight different animals can carry to the weight of each animal (e.g., a rhinoceros beetle can carry 160 pounds, but weighs three ounces).
- Students rank order the strength of the animals based on the ratio of their carrying ability (weight) to their size (weight).

Explain

The *Explain* stage is the third stage of the 5E Model. This stage encourages students to explain concepts and definitions in their own words. Students are asked to justify and clarify their ideas. Formal definitions, explanations, and labels are provided. The Explain stage is accomplished through activities

Critical Look-Fors

- Encourages students to work together without direct instruction from the teacher
- Promotes student dialogue as they interact
- Redirects students' investigations based on questions posed by themselves or others
- Provides time for students to puzzle through problems

such as discussions, small group instruction, video, or multimedia presentations and can include Socratic dialog or direct instruction, depending on the readiness level of the students.

Sample Math Lesson: Explanation Activities

- Students needing additional assistance with ratios complete a learning center activity using the video *Khan Academy: Introduction to Ratios.*
- The teacher organizes a set of math skill builders focusing on ratios as a review activity for students.

Critical Look-Fors

- Encourages students to explain concepts and definition in their own words
- Asks for justification (evidence) and clarification from students
- Formally provides definitions, explanations, and new labels
- Uses students' previous experiences as the basis for explaining concepts

Critical Look-Fors

- Expects students to use formal labels, definitions, and explanations provided previously
- Encourages students to apply or extend concepts and skills in new situations
- Reminds students of alternative explanations
- Refers students to existing data and evidence and asks, "What do you already know?" "Why do you think . . . ?"

Elaborate

The fourth stage of the 5E Model, *Elaborate*, allows students to apply their new processes, definitions, and skills in new but similar situations. It often involves experimental inquiry, investigative projects, and problem solving and decision making relating to the content under investigation as well as the lesson's culminating performance task.

Sample Math Lesson: Elaboration Activities

- Students decide which animal is the most athletic for its size based on the following criteria: strength (what they can carry), speed, leaping ability, and endurance.
- Students make their comparisons based on the ratio of each criterion to the size of the animal using common units.
- Students work in groups of three to complete a decision-making matrix

about the most athletic animal based on their research findings from the Internet and the corresponding ratios generated from their data.

Evaluate

The *Evaluate* stage is the final stage of the 5E Model and includes a wide variety of informal and formal assessment strategies. Teachers frequently observe students as they apply new concepts and skills to assess students' knowledge and/or skills, looking for evidence that the students have changed their thinking or behaviors. The opportunity to allow students to assess their own learning and group-process skills is often observed at this stage.

Sample Math Lesson: Evaluation Activities

- Students complete an exit card to articulate what they had learned from the learning experience.
- Students complete an online peer review assessment to assess the performance of their peers while working in pairs and in small groups based on scoring criteria generated by the students.

The 5E Model enables students to apply their learning to a real-world situation. In this way, the model readily supports additional Digital Age Best Practices (e.g., making authentic connections, differentiated instruction, digital tools and resources) while providing the classroom teacher with the needed flexibility to loop back into the 5E Learning Cycle depending on student readiness levels. Figures 1.0 and 1.1 include a sample elementary and secondary lesson plan that aligns with the 5E format and the Common Core State Standards (CCSS).

Critical Look-Fors

- Observes students as they apply new concepts and skills
- Assesses students' knowledge and/or skills
- Looks for evidence that students have challenged their thinking or behaviors
- Allows students to assess their own learning and group process skills

---

Figure 1.0   Lesson Plan: Extreme Weather

Fifth Grade

Extreme Weather

Teacher's Notes: Elementary 5E Reading Investigation

Common Core State Standards: Reading: Informational Text

(Continued)

Figure 1.0 (Continued)

RI.5.2 Determine two or more main ideas of a text and explain how they are supported by key details; summarize the text.

RI.5.3 Explain the relationships or interactions between two or more individuals, events, ideas, or concepts in a historical, scientific, or technical text based on specific information in the text.

RI.5.4 Determine the meaning of general academic and domain-specific words and phrases in a text relevant to a *Grade 5 topic or subject area*.

RI.5.5 Compare and contrast the overall structure (e.g., chronology, comparison, cause/effect, problem/solution) of events, ideas, concepts, or information in two or more texts.

RI.5.7 Draw on information from multiple print or digital sources, demonstrating the ability to locate an answer to a question quickly or to solve a problem efficiently.

RI.5.10 By the end of the year, read and comprehend informational texts, including history/social studies, science, and technical texts, at the high end of the Grades 4 through 5 text complexity band independently and proficiently.

5E Model—Engagement (Focus)

Estimated Time: Fifteen minutes

Driving Question: Who or what is causing the flooding?

Proposed Procedure:

Step 1: Show the following video clip in Slide 3 from the Extreme Weather PowerPoint highlighting recent flooding in Australia called *Toowoomba Flood* (http://www.youtube.com/watch?v=k YUpkPTcqPY). Ask students if they are in any way responsible for the severe flooding in Australia even though they live in the United States. If they believe they are responsible in any way, have them stand up.

Note: *If necessary, use Google Earth to show students the distance from their school to the location of this flood, Toowoomba, Australia.*

Step 2: On the whiteboard, write down students' reasons for impacting or not impacting the flooding in different parts of the world.

Step 3: Share with students that most climate scientists believe that every person on the planet is indirectly responsible for the wild weather occurring throughout the world because of the increase in the greenhouse effect. The greenhouse effect is the warming of the Earth's atmosphere caused by the increase in greenhouse gases trapping more of the Sun's heat, which would otherwise radiate from Earth.

Differentiation: Have students work in small groups with chart paper and markers. Divide chart paper into two sections: What do you believe impacts climate change, and what has no effect on climate change? Post chart papers around the room to share.

5E Model—Exploration

Estimated Time: Twenty minutes

Essential Question: What is the greenhouse effect?

Proposed Procedure:

Step 1: Have students work in collaborative groups to complete the following simple experiment to illustrate the greenhouse effect:

- Line a large open bowl with dark cloth or colored paper.
- Place the bowl in the sun and put an inverted paper cup in the bowl.
- Lay a thermometer across the top of the cup so that you are measuring the air temperature in the bowl.
- Note the temperature.
- Cover the bowl with a sheet of clear plastic wrap.
- Note the temperature reading after fifteen minutes compared to the temperature reading outside the bowl. The increase in air temperature is because of the trapped heat (Randall, 2013).

Step 2: Have students process why the temperature inside the bowl was higher than outside the bowl.

Step 3: Have each collaborative group share their collective responses from their observations using an online sticky note website such as Wallwisher (www.wallwisher.com).

Note: Remind students that the experiment was set up to model how greenhouse gases trap heat, thus increasing the temperature of the planet.

5E Model—Explanation

Estimated Time: Twenty minutes

Essential Question: How does global warming affect global climate?

(Continued)

Figure 1.0 (Continued)

Proposed Procedure:

Step 1: Have students participate in a practice reading assessment activity that focuses on reading comprehension relating to global warming and climate change while reinforcing critical CCSS-related reading standards addressing key ideas and details, craft and structure, integration of knowledge and ideas, and range of reading and level of text complexity.

Step 2: Use the Wordle-generated word cloud found on Slide 4 as a pre-reading exercise to get students thinking about the content of the text passage focusing on extreme weather called *Extreme Weather*.

Note: As you implement the reading benchmark intervention, it is suggested that the following sequence be used to accommodate the cross-spectrum of readers in your classroom ranging from dependent to independent readers.

Have the teacher read aloud the first section of the passage to the students. Afterward, have students, within a small collaborative group or large group, respond to specific questions embedded in the passage about different story elements of this section, focusing on one or more reading comprehension (e.g., cause and effect, main idea, drawing conclusions) and/or meta-cognitive (e.g., using context clues, looking for bolded words, doing think aloud) skills.

Note: It is strongly suggested that students use some form of digital responders/digital voters so their collective responses can be viewed quickly by the entire class. This affords the opportunity to discuss with students some of the major distracter answers embedded in the practice reading assessment.

Have students whisper or mumble read the next section as the teacher reads the text aloud. Afterward, have students respond to specific questions embedded in the passage about different story elements of this section within a small collaborative group or large group focusing on one or more reading comprehension and/or meta-cognitive skills.

Next, have students read silently the last section of the reading selection followed by prompted questions about the different story elements of this section, within a small collaborative group or large group, using one or more reading comprehension and/or meta-cognitive skills.

Step 3: Have students use the cause and effect graphic organizer (Handout 1) to trace the cause and effect trail from themselves as individuals to the global environment.

5E Model—Elaboration

Estimated Time: Thirty minutes

Essential Question: How can we reduce greenhouse gases?

Proposed Procedure:

Step 1: Show students different websites that enable individuals to calculate how much greenhouse gas they are personally responsible for that enters the Earth's atmosphere. These websites include

- U.S. Environmental Protection Agency: Climate Change—Greenhouse Gas Emissions

  http://www.epa.gov/climatechange/emissions/ind_calculator.html

- The Nature Conservancy: Carbon Footprint Calculator

  http://www.nature.org/greenliving/carboncalculator/

Step 2: Model for students how either calculator works for their household, then have them access one of the links to determine their personal impact on the environment.

Step 3: Have students work in collaborative groups to brainstorm different ways they can reduce their personal greenhouse gas contribution by accessing one or more of the websites below:

- Environmental Issues

  http://environment.about.com/od/globalwarming/tp/globalwarm tips.htm

- Natural-Environment.com

  http://www.natural-environment.com/

- Reduce Your Greenhouse Emissions

  http://www.wikihow.com/Reduce-Your-Greenhouse-Gas-Emissions

Step 4: Have students use an online decision-making matrix to determine the best strategy to reduce their personal and collective greenhouse gas contributions.

5E Model—Evaluation

Estimated Time: Five minutes

Essential Question: What did I learn about global warming and climate change?

Proposed Procedure:

Step 1: Have students complete the Exit Card in Handout 2.

Note: Access the handouts and PowerPoint slides for this lesson at http://www.lqhome.com/documents.

Figure 1.1   Lesson Plan: Heat Loss and Numerical Operations

Seventh Grade

Heat Loss and Numerical Operations

Teacher's Notes: 5E Math Investigation

Common Core State Standards:

7.NS.A.2. Apply and extend previous understandings of multiplication and division and of fractions to multiply and divide rational numbers.

7.NS.3. Solve real-world and mathematical problems involving the four operations with rational numbers.

5E Model—Engagement (Focus)

Estimated Time: Ten minutes

Driving Question: How much heat do we lose?

Proposed Procedure:

Step 1: Show students the video clip, *Heat Loss in a House,* to gain some perspective on how heat energy is wasted in our homes.

Step 2: Discuss with students the concept of heating degree days and *R*-values.

Note: In simple terms, a heating degree day represents the number of degrees that a day's average temperature is below 65° Fahrenheit (18° Celsius)—the temperature below which a building such as a school, house, or apartment needs to be heated. The R-value measures the ability for the insulation inside a building's walls to resist heat flow. The higher your R-value is, the more effective your insulation.

Step 3: Have students complete an energy conservation quiz on Slides 3 through 8 from the *Heat Loss and Operations* PowerPoint to reflect on their personal lifestyle choices

5E Model—Exploration

Estimated Time: Fifteen minutes

Essential Question: Can I calculate heat loss?

Proposed Procedure:

Note: Students will calculate the heat loss from conduction and infiltration in their classroom.

Step 1: Have students work in collaborative groups using Handout 1 to record the surface area of the walls, windows, and ceiling of their classroom in Table 1.

Step 2: Have students use the *R*-values in Handout 2 to estimate the *R*-values of the surface area and record the results in Table 1 in Handout 1.

Step 3: Have students retrieve the heating degree days for their region by accessing the website BizEE Degree Days and enter the information in Table 2 in Handout 1.

Step 4: Have students calculate the heat loss from conduction by using the following equation:

Heat Loss From Conduction

$$\text{Heat Loss} = \left(\frac{1}{R - \text{value}}\right) \times \text{Surface Area} \times 24 \text{ hours} \times \text{DD}$$

Note: *The above equation assumes the following:*

- *A heating degree day takes into account both the difference in temperature between the inside and outside air and the time.*
- *The number of degree hours for your heating season can be computed by multiplying the number of degree days by 24.*
- *Conductivity is the inverse of resistance and can be expressed as $\frac{1}{R}$.*
- *DD represents degree days.*

Step 4: Have students use Table 3 in Handout 1 to record the length, width, and height of their classroom.

Step 5: Have students calculate the volume of air space (ft^3) in Table 4.

Step 6: Have students use the air turnovers in Handout 2 to estimate the number of air turnovers per hour and record the information in Table 4 in Handout 1.

Step 7: Have students calculate the heat loss from infiltration by using the following equation:

Heat Loss From Infiltration

$$\text{Heat Loss} = \text{Volume} \times 0.018 \times N \times 24 \times \text{DD}$$

Note: *The above equation assumes the following:*

- *The volume of air in a classroom can be found by measuring the volume of air space within the classroom.*

(Continued)

Figure 1.1 (Continued)

- N *represents the number of air turnovers per hour, which can be estimated using Handout 1.*
- *The quantity, 0.018 Btu/ft³/Fahrenheit, represents the heat required to raise the temperature of 1 cubic foot of air through 1 degree Fahrenheit.*
- *DD represents degree days.*

Step 8: Within their collaborative groups, have students evaluate the results of their calculations as well as conduct a peer evaluation form for each participant in their group.

5E Model—Explanation

Estimated Time: Twenty minutes

Essential Question: How can I follow the algebraic order of operations?

Proposed Procedure:

Step 1: Have students respond to the questions on Slides 9 through 11 from the *Heat Loss and Operations* PowerPoint.

Differentiation: Have the group of students needing additional assistance with algebraic order of operations complete a learning center activity. Allow them to work through any one of the following interactive applets to reinforce their understanding of mathematical operations:

- Kahn Academy—Order of Operations

  http://www.khanacademy.org/video/introduction-to-order-of-operations?playlist=Pre-algebra

- Kahn Academy—Order of Operations

  http://www.khanacademy.org/video/order-of-operations?playlist=Developmental%20Math

- Order of Operations

  http://www.math.com/school/subject2/lessons/S2U1L2GL.html

Note: It is suggested that you use the Benchmark 1 Math Skill Builders as well as mental math and "mad minute" activities to review and/or reinforce mathematical operations.

5E Model—Elaboration

Estimated Time: Open-ended

Essential Question: How can I reduce heat loss?

Proposed Procedure:

Step 1: Have students discuss strategies for reducing heat loss at school or in their homes by accessing any of the websites below:

- Tips on Saving Energy by Reducing Heat Loss

  http://www.hammerzone.com/archives/energy/conservation/basics_1/tips.htm
- Saving Energy

  http://www.energyquest.ca.gov/saving_energy/index.html
- Wintertime Energy Savings Tips

  http://www.consumerenergycenter.org/tips/winter.html

Step 2: Have students working in collaborative groups use the equations for heat loss from conduction and infiltration to estimate the amount of heat energy saved annually by implementing one or more heat reduction strategies.

Step 3: Have students brainstorm and select the most viable solution for reducing heat loss at a targeted building on campus.

5E Model—Evaluation

Estimated Time: Five minutes

Essential Question: What did I learn about algebraic order of operations?

Proposed Procedure:

Step 1: Have students complete the Exit Card in Handout 3.

Note: Access the handouts and PowerPoint slides for this lesson at http://www.lqhome.com/documents.

Implementation Challenges

In theory, the use of the 5E Model or 5E Learning Cycle as a concrete strategy to support Digital Age Best Practices seems obvious. Building lesson plans with a high level of fidelity to the model ensures that the learner will be given the opportunity to generate meaningful questions (Engage), explore concepts/processes through group collaboration (Explore), and apply their learning to an authentic situation (Elaborate). The model also aligns with a LoTi 3 implementation where the instructional focus emphasizes student higher-order thinking (i.e., analyzing, evaluating, creating) and engaged learning. At a LoTi 3, digital tools and/or environmental resources are used by students to carry out teacher-directed tasks that emphasize higher levels of student cognitive processing relating to the content under investigation.

In reality, the actual use of the 5E Model in the Atlantic City Public Schools presented several potential challenges to its successful implementation including the prospect of teacher resistance because of a required shift in the conventional teaching paradigm, confrontation with the teacher's union, insufficient building level support, and a lack of teacher efficacy. Anyone of these barriers could have minimized the model's impact on the instructional curriculum and ultimately, on student learning opportunities in the classroom. The district's leadership team executed a set of strategies aimed at keeping all stakeholders focused on the innovation and not the potential negativity associated with its implementation.

Grassroots Support

What the district did early in the implementation was to create grassroots interest and support for the 5E Model at its summer teacher institutes focusing on a single content area (i.e., mathematics). At these institutes, teachers participated in experiential learning episodes playing the role of "students" within a series of simulated 5E math lessons. Afterward, the summer participants debriefed about their experiences, either as teachers modeling a 5E lesson or as students. The result helped to provide the crucial "buy-in" to the model as a means of bolstering student engagement and academic performance.

Online Professional Development

An online Moodle course entitled *The 5E Model* was developed in-house by district personnel to provide staff with an asynchronous outlet to get collegial feedback about their own use of the model. District literacy and math coaches were also available to provide in-class modeling of the 5E Model at the target LoTi 3 implementation.

Staff Empowerment

The district was equally proactive in troubleshooting potential problems regarding the adoption of a structured lesson plan model.

Since state CAPA (Collaborative Assessment for Planning and Achievement) guidelines required teachers to maintain a hard copy of their daily lesson plans, the district sought feedback from staff as to ways of streamlining the 5E lesson template so as to address the needs of different grade level and/or content area teachers. Representatives of the teacher union were consulted regularly throughout the lesson plan development process to ensure that all key stakeholders were aware of the pending changes to the lesson plan format.

District-Approved Curriculum

District leadership also integrated the requirement for online lessons into the Atlantic City Public Schools Instructional Plan. Since this plan required board approval, the requirement of posting weekly 5E lesson plans online became de facto board policy, thus making the 5E lesson posting a nonunion issue. This step helped change the conversation from a possible union issue over lesson plan requirements and the subsequent negative publicity to a focus on challenging staff to improve student engagement and real-world problem solving in the classroom.

SUMMARY

This chapter opened with a scene from a conventional teacher-centered social studies classroom where the lesson objectives, corresponding standards, and essential questions were clearly articulated by the teacher to his or her students. Within a standards-based curriculum, generating an essential question to guide student learning theoretically gives students an advanced organizer in which to track their learning associated with the content under investigation. In practice, most essential questions fall on deaf ears because they have not been properly contextualized by the learner.

Simply inscribing the essential question on an interactive whiteboard or casually referencing it during a lesson episode fails to give students proper and needed relevancy to contextualize its meaning. Comparing the causes of the American Revolution to a "breakup" letter between a boyfriend and girlfriend provided students with a valuable anchor in which to conceptualize why British citizens would want to revolt against their own government.

The 5E Model epitomizes this approach—an approach embedded in digital age teaching and learning and specifically the Digital Age

Best Practice *Bolstering purposeful inquiry through student questions* by providing educators with an effective way to organize instruction so that students can generate purposeful questions and solve problems authentically relating to the content.

As we have learned, great innovations in education are not always implemented—not because they lack merit or integrity on their own to improve instruction and student learning, but because they have become fodder for personal or group agendas unrelated to the goal of continuous improvement. As we explore Chapter 2 and its focus on the Digital Age Best Practice *Promoting shared expertise with networked collaboration*, consider the following questions:

- How would you characterize the dominant instructional practices in your school setting or classroom?
- What variables impede or restrict the role of 21st Century Skills in the classroom?
- What professional development either onsite, online, or blended is currently in place that can promote collaborative learning environments?

2

Promoting Shared Expertise With Networked Collaboration

Probably the best way to understand networked collaboration is to borrow a few lines from the famous Ron Howard–directed movie, *Apollo 13*. At one point in the movie, the audience witnesses NASA scientists, engineers, and contractors frantically attempting to save the lives of the three astronauts by building a makeshift CO_2 filter out of materials aboard the lunar module *Aquarius*. As mission control flight director Gene Kranz, played by actor Ed Harris, issues the directive, "We must find a way to make a square plug fit into a round hole rapidly," the audience hears what amounts to a loosely coupled culminating performance task issued from one of the NASA department heads, "We got to find a way to make this fit into the hole for that using nothing but that [miscellaneous space equipment]!"

Watching the ensemble of NASA personnel feverishly discussing design options, performing trial and error experiments, and articulating the steps leading to a solution to save the ill-fated astronauts represents the pinnacle of networked collaboration. Networked collaboration or collaborative learning goes beyond having two or more students seated near one another working in isolation. Instead it represents a synergistic effort to solve a self-generated problem or perhaps one issued by the teacher (e.g., Mr. Jimenez is building a wooden deck in his backyard. How much decking material in terms of 2 × 6s will he need to construct a deck with the following dimensions: 15 feet by 24 feet. What would you recommend as to the type of decking [e.g., redwood, Douglas fir, cedar, composite] based on the per foot cost?).

Collaborative learning encompasses five primary steps:

1. Defining a problem in terms of needs

2. Brainstorming possible solutions

3. Selecting a solution

4. Executing a plan of action or solution

5. Evaluating the plan of action or solution

Using the math example above, students working in teams of four complete the following steps within a collaborative learning environment:

1. Defining the Problem in Terms of Needs

Students would collaborate to reach a consensus as to the agree-upon problem by asking their teacher, Mr. Jimenez, probing questions; creating a T-Chart outlining both the known and unknown information about the problem; and/or clarifying their understanding of the problem within their collaborative group. The problem in this situation is twofold: (1) determining the amount of decking material (redwood, cedar, Douglas fir, composite) needed to complete the backyard deck and (2) calculating the total cost of the decking material.

2. Brainstorming Possible Solutions

Students openly discuss different strategies for solving the backyard deck problem within their collaborative group. Possible solutions might be determining the type of climate and decking options consistent with the amount of precipitation or inclement weather for the targeted area and conducting a cost comparison between different types of decking material.

3. Selecting a Possible Solution

Two members of one of the collaborative teams decide to access *The Weather Channel* (www.weather.com) and investigate the climate for the targeted area. The remaining two members of the collaborative team decide to use an online decision-making matrix to conduct a cost comparison among the competing types of decking.

4. Executing a Plan of Action or Solution

Both pairs of students complete their respective investigation, arrive at the optimum material for decking based on climate as well as per unit cost, and then determine the actual cost for the decking material based on their collective recommendation.

5. Evaluating a Plan of Action or Solution

Students working in their collaborative group use a class-generated scoring guide to assess the accuracy of their solution as well as a peer-review rubric to assess individual and group participation in the activity.

One website that best encapsulates the tenets of networked collaboration is eCybermission (www.ecybermission.com). Because this website hosts a competition where students work in small groups to solve science, technology, engineering, and mathematics (STEM) problems, it is an ideal real-world connection that brings together student interests, key content objectives, and opportunities for problem solving and decision making that goes beyond the confines of the classroom. The role of networked collaboration is an integral part of the problem-solving/decision-making process. A brief synopsis of some of these projects from the eCybermission website appears in Figure 2.0.

As you review the sample eCybermission projects, several critical look-fors of networked collaboration are apparent: (1) emphasis on issues resolution or problem solving, (2) student inquiry, (3) collaborative decision making, and (4) real-world connections. Each of the sample projects is also an example of a LoTi 5: Expansion. At a Level 5 (Expansion), student collaborations extending beyond the classroom are employed for authentic problem solving and issues resolution.

Critical Look-Fors

- Emphasis on issues resolution or problem solving
- Student inquiry
- Collaborative decision making
- Real-world connections

Emphasis is placed on learner-centered strategies that promote personal goal setting and self-monitoring, student action, and collaborations with other groups (e.g., another school, different cultures, business establishments, governmental agencies) using the available digital tools and/or environmental resources.

Figure 2.0   Descriptions of eCybermission Winning Projects

Grade 6: Hardheads. The Hardheads team was recognized by judges for their experiments with materials used to support sports helmets. For their project, the students conducted experiments on multiple materials for possible use in sports helmets, with the hope of finding a material that decreases the prevalence of concussions and other head injuries. The team tested foam, neoprene rubber, and gel rubber, to identify a material that could yield a safer, form-fitting helmet that is more effective than the foam-insulated helmets currently in use. The students determined that gel rubber was far more shock absorbent than foam and contacted multiple helmet manufacturers requesting that they explore the viable alternative.

Grade 7: Blue Starz. To help in the preservation of gopher tortoises, which are threatened by urbanization, disease, hunting, and low reproductive potential, the Blue Starz team conducted experiments to calculate the number of gopher tortoise burrows in a nearby wildlife sanctuary. They contacted representatives from their state's fish and wildlife conservation commission, including environmental specialists at their local wildlife sanctuary, and used surveying techniques and GPS technology to locate existing burrows, calculate the total number of gopher tortoises and burrows in the sanctuary, and calculate the number of additional gopher tortoises the sanctuary could accept for protection.

Grade 8: 'Cane Hammers. Because of the prevalence of hurricanes in the area, the 'Cane Hammers wanted to identify the type of mobile home roof that is most resistant to wind. The team constructed a wind tunnel and tested various roof shapes to determine which type could best withstand the wind. The students concluded that sloped roofs are most effective, and therefore mobile homes and other portable structures should not be built with flat roofs. The team plans to communicate their findings to mobile home construction companies and residents in their community.

Grade 9: Bioquadrant. Recognizing that deer play an important part in the food chain, the Bioquadrant team was concerned about reports in the media regarding the health of Virginia's wild deer population. The team conducted experiments on deer liver tissue to determine mineral composition and completed a soil sample mineral analysis to determine the relationship between the soil and the deer tissue. As a result of their research, the team hopes to supply the deer population in their area with mineral supplements.

Practical Application

The use of the Digital Age Best Practice *Promoting shared expertise with networked collaboration* can be retrofitted into any K–12 classroom. In the Atlantic City Public Schools, the use of the 5E Model provided a natural segue for networked collaboration in the classroom. Two stages of the 5E Model in particular, Exploration and Elaboration, easily promote collaborative learning as students attempt to make connections and explore new concepts at the Exploration stage and then apply or transfer their learning to a new situation (often with consequences) at the Elaboration stage.

Figures 2.1 and 2.2 highlight sections of sample 5E lessons used in reading and mathematics, respectively, that emphasize collaborative learning within the Exploration and Expansion sections of the model.

Figure 2.1   Lesson Plan: Bill of Rights, Grade 5

Grade 5

Bill of Rights

Teacher's Notes: 5E Reading Investigation

Common Core State Standards:

CCSS.ELA-Literacy.RI.5.1 Quote accurately from a text when explaining what the text says explicitly and when drawing inferences from the text.

CCSS.ELA-Literacy.RI.5.2 Determine two or more main ideas of a text and explain how they are supported by key details; summarize the text.

CCSS.ELA-Literacy.RI.5.3 Explain the relationships or interactions between two or more individuals, events, ideas, or concepts in a historical, scientific, or technical text based on specific information in the text.

CCSS.ELA-Literacy.RI.5.4 Determine the meaning of general academic and domain-specific words and phrases in a text relevant to a *Grade 5 topic or subject area*.

5E Model—Exploration

Estimated Time: Fifteen minutes

Guiding Question: Which rights are most important?

(Continued)

Figure 2.1 (Continued)

Proposed Procedure:

Step 1: Show a video of a jet landing on a distant island in Slide 2 of the *Bill of Rights* PowerPoint. Tell students that their entire class has decided to move to this faraway island to start a new country.

Step 2: Have students discuss what rights individual students should be entitled to as citizens of this island. Record student responses on the whiteboard.

Step 3: Distribute Handout 1 describing fifteen human rights that were mentioned by their peers during their long flight to this distant island.

Step 4: Working in small groups, have students prioritize their top ten rights that should be considered as the foundation for a new government on the island based on this original list of fifteen rights.

Note: *For convenience, these fifteen human rights can be set up as an online survey, such as Survey Monkey (www.surveymonkey.com), so that students can quickly view the aggregate results after they have finished prioritizing their preferred list of human rights.*

Step 5: Prompt students in their groups to identify any patterns or trends relating to the tabulated data. Which human rights were most preferred by students? Which human rights were least preferred by students?

Step 6: Share with students that a similar process took place over two hundred years ago when a series of constitutional amendments called the Bill of Rights were ratified by the states limiting the power of the U.S. federal government and protecting the natural rights of all citizens.

5E Model—Elaboration

Estimated Time: Fifteen minutes

Essential Question: What are my rights as a student?

Proposed Procedure:

Step 1: Distribute individual Bill of Rights cards from Handout 2 to students assembled in small groups. Have each group review the card and rewrite the original text in everyday language that everyone can understand. Next, have all students perform a gallery walk to give feedback to the rewritten text from each group.

Sample Card

Fifth Amendment

No person shall . . . be subject for

the same offense to be twice

put in jeopardy of life of limb.

Differentiation: Divide students into groups of four. Distribute Bill of Right Cards from website, US Constitution Online (http://www.usconstitution.net/consttop_stud.html), and have students match up the meanings of the Bill of Rights. Discuss together.

Step 2: Have students in groups of three investigate the individual rights afforded them as students in a public school. How are these rights similar or different than the rights given to all citizens under the Constitution? Are any of these rights being violated? Use the following website as a reference: US Constitution Online (http://www.usconstitution.net/consttop_stud.html).

Note: Access the handouts and PowerPoint slides for this lesson at http://www.lqhome.com/documents.

Figure 2.2   Lesson Plan: Crime and Transformations

Grade 8

Crime and Transformations

Teacher's Notes: 5E Math Investigation

Common Core State Standards:

CCSS.Math.Content.8.G.A.3 Describe the effect of dilations, translations, rotations, and reflections on two-dimensional figures using coordinates.

5E Model—Exploration

Estimated Time: Fifteen minutes

Guiding Question: Where are the police patrols?

(Continued)

Figure 2.2 (Continued)

Proposed Procedure:

Step 1: Have students work in groups of three to identify and record the ordered pairs of "police patrols" for different locations in the downtown San Diego area. Handout 1 displays a two-dimensional coordinate grid over downtown San Diego, California.

Note: *Use this activity to find out students' proficiency level with locating points on an x/y coordinate grid.*

Step 2: Have students identify the ordered pairs for the location of each law enforcement patrol in Handout 1. Use Slides 12 through 20 from the *Crime and Transformations* PowerPoint to review the location of the law enforcement patrols on the two-dimensional coordinate grid over downtown San Diego.

Step 3: Distribute Handout 2 for students to work in groups of three to plot the location of criminal activity for different locations in the downtown San Diego area. Have them plot Points A to F on the map in Handout 1B based on the ordered pairs provided in Handout 2.

Step 4: Use Slides 21 through 28 from the *Crime and Transformations* PowerPoint to review the actual coordinate points for each criminal act in San Diego.

Step 5: Have students respond to questions about current and future criminal activity trends based on their coordinate grid using Slides 29 through 46 from the *Crime and Transformations* PowerPoint.

5E Model—Elaboration

Estimated Time: Fifteen minutes

Driving Question: What if the crime areas change?

Proposed Procedure:

Step 1: Have each student group use Handout 3 to respond to question prompts about current and future criminal activity trends based on their ordered pairs using the *Crime and Transformations* PowerPoint Slides 47 through 71.

Note: *In this section, students will be performing transformations (i.e., reflection, translation) of criminal acts and then making decisions as to where to reposition local law enforcement patrols.*

Step 2: Based on their hypotheses about future criminal activity, have each group of students reposition the police patrols on the San Diego Crime Map using ordered pairs (*Crime Fighters* PowerPoint Slides 72–76). Have students explain their responses.

Note: Access the handouts and PowerPoint slides for this lesson at http://www .lqhome.com/documents.

Both of these 5E lessons illustrate key attributes of networked or collaborative learning at the Exploration and Expansion stages with their emphasis on group problem solving/decision making, consensus building, and social interaction. They also showcase the many residual benefits of collaborative learning in the classroom, including

- Increasing student retention
- Developing oral communication skills
- Promoting a positive attitude toward the content
- Exploring alternate problem solutions within a safe environment
- Aligning with a constructivist approach
- Encouraging student responsibility for learning
- Developing empathy for others
- Promoting alternative assessment techniques (Panitz, 2013)

Implementation Challenges

Though the 5E Model provides a useful medium in which to integrate the benefits of collaborative learning, the fidelity of implementation still rests with each teacher's existing schema for teaching and learning. Whereas teachers whose fundamental pedagogical style aligns with a learner-centered approach, the use of networked collaboration within the 5E Model appears transparent; however, teachers implementing a teacher-centered approach oftentimes struggle with the perceived lack of control inherent with group activities.

Still other variables may diminish the role of networked collaboration. Lack of self-confidence by teachers or a lack of familiarity with the cooperative learning model may restrict full-scale implementation. Concern with high stakes tests, classroom management, and a lack of prepared materials are additional factors cited where teachers may reject collaborative learning or any other student grouping facsimile.

Summer Literacy Institute

As mentioned earlier, generating grassroots support for any innovation is vital to its overall success. One strategy for eradicating potential barriers to networked collaboration was providing model lesson plans for staff members to use as anchors throughout the school year. In the Atlantic City Public Schools, a Summer Literacy Institute was implemented that brought together teams of literacy coaches for the purpose of creating model 5E lesson plans that (a) increased students' knowledge base in the fields of science and social studies, (b) integrated the tenets of collaborative learning, (c) focused on reading comprehension and metacognitive skill development especially in the areas of informational text, (d) promoted student engagement, and (e) provided practice assessments aligned to the state high stakes test.

Students from low socioeconomic areas do not oftentimes possess the same amount of prior knowledge via life experiences as students from a higher socioeconomic stratum. Since many state-administered reading assessments include nonfictional or informational passages, the Atlantic City Board of Education wanted to address this need especially in the area of informational text through the development of literacy-based 5E lessons.

In-Class Modeling

The model 5E lesson plans were modeled throughout the school year in the targeted classrooms providing teachers with an opportunity to observe networked collaboration in action as well as the other stages of the 5E Model. Staff witnessed firsthand how positive group dynamics in the form of collaborative learning can be used productively to achieve both academic rigor and relevance while addressing the need for prior knowledge acquisition, especially in the areas of science and social studies.

Classroom Walkthrough Form

The district classroom walkthrough form called *H.E.A.R.T.* (Higher-Order Thinking, Engaged Learning, Authentic Connections, Rubrics, Technology Use) included a specific set of look-fors addressing Engaged learning that indirectly reinforced the role of networked collaboration in the classroom. The Engaged learning section of the Atlantic City Board of Education walkthrough form appears below:

1. Students report what they have learned only.
2. Students collaborate to report what they have learned with possible options.
3. Students solve a teacher-directed problem.
4. Students collaborate to solve a teacher-directed problem with possible options.
5. Students collaborate to define the task, the process, and/or the solution.

6. Students collaborate to define the task, the process, and/or the solution; collaboration extends beyond the classroom.

SUMMARY

This chapter uses the events from the movie *Apollo 13* as the backdrop for introducing networked collaboration or collaborative learning. As in the movie, enabling students to work collaboratively to achieve a common goal based on the synergy generated from individual team members provides a multitude of academic benefits to both students and teachers.

However, collaboration in the classroom doesn't happen overnight. It consists of careful planning and execution in order to maximize its impact on the learner. Building the necessary capacity for the Digital Age Best Practice *Promoting shared expertise with networked collaboration* requires a district and building-level commitment to resource development (i.e., 5E lesson plans), professional learning (i.e., in-classroom modeling), and frequent monitoring (H.E.A.R.T. walkthroughs). Each of these areas is critical to overcoming obstacles to the change process.

The movie *Apollo 13* culminates with the three Apollo astronauts, James Lovell, Jack Swigert, and Fred Haise, making a safe splashdown of their command module *Odyssey* in the South Pacific as a result of hours of collaborative problem solving from NASA scientists, technicians, and contractors. As with the actual events of Apollo 13, executing a collaborative learning environment requires similar leadership skills at the classroom, building, and district levels to plan, organize, implement, and evaluate classroom learning experiences that leverage existing resources to achieve maximum student academic success.

The role of leadership is critical to the successful execution of each of the Digital Age Best Practices. As we explore Chapter 3 and its focus on the Digital Age Best Practice *Personalizing and globalizing content by making authentic connections*, consider the following questions:

- How can proactive leadership reduce possible barriers to successful innovation implementation?
- What strategies have you incorporated in your PLCs or district leadership meetings that minimize personal or group agendas?
- What role can 21st Century Skills/Themes assume in providing more authentic connections to students?

3

Personalizing and Globalizing Content by Making Authentic Connections

Figure 3.0 presents an all-too-familiar math probe of a fifth-grade classroom. This probe was administered to a heterogeneous group of students at an elementary school. In this math probe, students were orally read the following directions:

1. Fold a blank sheet of paper into four sections.

2. In the upper left corner box, draw one and one half.

3. In the upper right corner box, make a circle divided into eight sections. Color in three fourths of the circle.

4. In the lower left corner box, add the numbers three hundredths, thirty, and three.

5. In the lower right corner box, subtract one from a million.

We used this same probe with hundreds of other fifth-grade students throughout the country, all of which confirmed the following

Figure 3.0   Math Probe

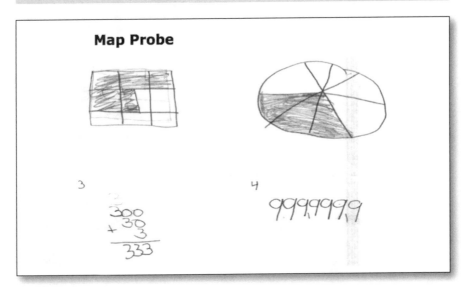

preconceived notions: (a) many students continue to struggle with number representation, (b) many students experience difficulty distinguishing between the word and number forms of fractions and whole numbers and subtracting multi-digit numbers, and (c) an overwhelming percentage of teachers swear they have covered the above math content repeatedly during the year as well as in prior years.

What causes a "deer in the headlights" phenomenon when students are asked a question in an unorthodox manner that does not precisely match the word length and format of a textbook problem? How can schools avoid the *IOEOTO* (In One Ear Out the Other) *Effect* as it relates to retention and transfer?

The answer lies in contextualizing the content so that students are able to make the necessary connections both internally and externally. Internal connections imply the students are able to connect multiple concepts that are often taught in isolation, such as in mathematics (e.g., fractions versus probability, ratio versus geometric shapes, algebraic equations versus statistics). Finding common links that enable students to visualize relationships and make long-term connections provide an efficient way to minimize the IOEOTO Effect in the classroom. Figures 3.1 and 3.2 demonstrate the transformation of isolated math content (e.g., warm-up activities A, B, and C) into a single contextualized content activity (e.g., math skill builder).

Figure 3.1   Consolidated isolated math concepts appearing on the left with a contextualized version of the same math concepts on the right deepens students understanding.

Isolated Content	Contextualized Content
Warm-Up Activity A	*Math Skill Builder: Grade 7*
Convert the following from a fraction to a decimal.	Maryanne is doing an experiment with her marble collection. She put four blue marbles, five green marbles, six yellow marbles, and one red marble in a bag.
$\dfrac{1}{3}$ _____	
$\dfrac{3}{4}$ _____	*Part A.* Write a fraction reduced to the lowest terms showing the probability of Maryanne choosing a blue marble without looking in the bag. Express the ratio of yellow to blue marbles in lowest terms.
$\dfrac{4}{16}$ _____	
Warm-Up Activity B	*Part B.* If she does not replace the blue marble in the bag, what is the probability of her choosing a blue marble on the second pick? Write your answer as a fraction, a decimal, and a percentage.
Write the following fractions in lowest terms.	
$\dfrac{4}{16}$ _____	
$\dfrac{3}{24}$ _____	
$\dfrac{16}{56}$ _____	
Warm-Up Activity C	
If you had a bag of marbles with four blue marbles, five green marbles, six yellow marbles, and one red marble, what would be the probability of drawing out the following?	
One blue marble? _____	
Two yellow marbles in a row if you replaced the first yellow marble after the first draw? _____	

Figure 3.2 Consolidated isolated math concepts appearing on the left with a contextualized version of the same math concepts on the right deepens students understanding.

Isolated Content	Contextualized Content
Warm-Up Activity A	*Math Problem-of-the-Day: Grade 8*

Warm-Up Activity A

Complete the ratio problems below.

Five has what ratio to 15? _____

Ten has what ratio to 100? _____

Warm-Up Activity B

Answer the questions below.

1. A map is drawn with a scale of 1 cm on the map representing 2 km. What is the actual length of the lake that is 4 cm long? _____

2. If the scale of the hotel map is 1 cm: 10 m, what is the distance from the highway to the hotel if on the map it is 3 cm long? _____

Warm-Up Activity C

Complete the steps below.

1. Plot four points (A, B, C, D) on the coordinate grid to form a rectangle.

2. What are the four coordinates?

   A = _____ B = _____

   C = _____ D = _____

Math Problem-of-the-Day: Grade 8

Rectangle P, Q, R, S will be dilated with the origin as the center of dilation to form rectangle P′, Q′, R′, S′.

- If the scale factor is .5 from the original, how many units long will line segment P′S′ be? _____

- What is the ratio of the area of the dilated rectangle to the area of the original rectangle? _____

- Reflect the dilated rectangle over the *x*-axis. What are the four coordinates of the reflected rectangle? _____

   P′ = _____ Q′ = _____

   R′ = _____ S′ = _____

In some instances, professional educators may, at first, be confused as to what seems to be some unnatural connections among math concepts (e.g., integrating algebraic reasoning with data analysis), but upon closer inspection, the internal connections not only make sense but help students contextualize the content. For example, developing an understanding of fractions is a prerequisite for exploring probability, mixing ratios with geometric shapes extends students' understanding of number representation, and linking algebraic reasoning with statistics strikes at the core of data analysis or the ability to gather, organize, display, and analyze data.

External connections represent students transferring or applying the content to a real-world or authentic situation that possesses potential consequences; 21st Century Themes provide a convenient way to form these external connections by employing one or more themes to a specific concept or skill. As mentioned in an earlier chapter, these 21st Century Themes include global awareness; financial, economic, business, and entrepreneurial literacy; civic literacy; health literacy; and environmental literacy. A succinct description of these 21st Century Themes from the *Partnership for 21st Century Skills* website follows.

Global Awareness

- Using 21st Century Skills to understand and address global issues
- Learning from and working collaboratively with individuals representing diverse cultures, religions, and lifestyles in a spirit of mutual respect and open dialogue in personal, work, and community contexts
- Understanding other nations and cultures, including the use of non-English languages

Financial, Economic, Business, and Entrepreneurial Literacy

- Knowing how to make appropriate personal economic choices
- Understanding the role of the economy in society
- Using entrepreneurial skills to enhance workplace productivity and career options

Civic Literacy

- Participating effectively in civic life through knowing how to stay informed and understanding governmental processes

- Exercising the rights and obligations of citizenship at local, state, national, and global levels
- Understanding the local and global implications of civic decisions

Health Literacy

- Obtaining, interpreting, and understanding basic health information and services and using such information and services in ways that are health enhancing
- Understanding preventive physical and mental health measures, including proper diet, nutrition, exercise, risk avoidance, and stress reduction
- Using available information to make appropriate health-related decisions
- Establishing and monitoring personal and family health goals
- Understanding national and international public health and safety issues

Environmental Literacy

- Demonstrate knowledge and understanding of the environment and the circumstances and conditions affecting it, particularly as relates to air, climate, land, food, energy, water, and ecosystems
- Demonstrate knowledge and understanding of society's impact on the natural world (e.g., population growth, population development, resource consumption rate, etc.)
- Investigate and analyze environmental issues and make accurate conclusions about effective solutions
- Take individual and collective action toward addressing environmental challenges (e.g., participating in global actions, designing solutions that inspire action on environmental issues)

Practical Application

The use of the Digital Age Best Practice *Personalizing and globalizing content by making authentic connections* can be manifested in a multitude of ways based on grade level and content area. Following are sample lesson plan vignettes that integrate one or more 21st Century Themes.

Grade 3 Mathematics: Economic, Business, and Entrepreneurial Literacy

Getting young students to think about the entrepreneurial process at an early age can help strengthen math skills as well as motivate them to explore the foundation of free-market capitalism. Many of us experienced the lemonade stand venture as children in an attempt to achieve a profit from customers yearning for a reprieve from a long hot summer day.

In this activity, students explore the lemonade stand concept but then collaborate with their classmates to create and sell their own product to their peers at school as a way of applying two and three digit subtraction.

Grade 5 Literacy: Environmental Literacy

According to the U.S. Environmental Protection Agency, "In 2011, Americans generated about 250 million tons of trash and recycled and composted almost 87 million tons of this material, equivalent to a 34.7 percent recycling rate" (U.S. Environmental Protection Agency, 2013, p. 1). On average, the amount of individual waste generated by each person in the United States amounts to 4.40 pounds per day, of which 1.53 pounds of this total is recycled and composted.

In this activity, students gain background knowledge using informational text about worldwide garbage and its subsequent impact on the environment and then apply their understanding by creating viable solutions for minimizing the amount of trash destined for the local landfill.

Grade 7 Mathematics: Health Literacy

People live with risk around the clock. Statisticians tell us that there is a mathematical risk with everything we do, from walking to the local convenience store on a weekday to traveling to work each morning. There are even potential health risks at home, stemming from such phenomena as radon, electromagnetic fields, and from asbestos in the ceiling.

In this activity, students examine the concept of probability as it relates to different job risks and conduct their own risk assessment for careers of their choice. Afterward, they complete a decision-making matrix for their ideal career based on a series of variables, including risk, salary, popularity, and danger.

Grade 8 Literacy: Global Awareness

The Amistad, also known as *United States v. Libellants and Claimants of the Schooner Amistad*, 40 U.S. (15 Pet.) 518 (1841), was a U.S. Supreme Court case resulting from the rebellion of slaves on board the Spanish schooner Amistad in 1839. The rebellion broke out when the schooner, traveling along the coast of Cuba, was taken over by a group of captives who had earlier been kidnapped in Africa and sold into slavery. Later, the Supreme Court confirmed that the Africans were entitled to take whatever legal measures necessary to secure their freedom, including the use of force.

In this activity, students will gather background knowledge about the Amistad and then apply their understanding of slavery to child slavery and human trafficking practices occurring today throughout the world.

Implementation Challenges

Few people would argue about the benefits of integrating 21st Century Themes into the K–12 curriculum. Providing a real-world context, promoting group collaboration, and offering a rich context for applied learning are all positive consequences of authentic learning opportunities. As referenced earlier in this book, the evidence supporting the Digital Age Best Practice *Personalizing and globalizing content by making authentic connections* is substantial; yet the practice of creating learning environments that capitalize on this best practice is minimal. Why?

Informal interviews and queries within the teaching ranks often cite lack of time, interference with the established scope and sequence or curriculum map matrix, lack of available resources, inadequate professional development, and concerns about the Common Core State Standards (CCSS). Each one of these concerns individually or collectively could undermine any attempt at promoting 21st Century Themes. In the Atlantic City Public Schools, procedures and programs were established early in the implementation process that would negate any one of these concerns.

Model Lessons

The Atlantic City Board of Education enlisted the assistance of their reading coaches, grade-level teachers, and supervisors to design exemplary literacy investigations that would meet the following criteria: (a) promote a high level of H.E.A.R.T. applied to student learning, (b) integrate one or more 21st Century Themes, (c) include practice reading assessments that emphasized informational text aligned to the CCSS, and (d) promote the 5E Model.

During the pilot stage a total of sixteen model literacy lessons were created for each grade level in Grades 5 through 8 focusing on informational text drawn from the science and social studies content. All lesson plans and accompanying multimedia presentations, video links, and resources were also housed at the district online resource site for easy access. Grade-level teachers were given an opportunity to pilot test each literacy lesson for their grade level and then collaborate with their colleagues to integrate each of the sixteen model lessons into their respective curriculum maps.

Professional Development

In concert with the model literacy lessons, job-embedded modeling of targeted fifth- through eighth-grade classrooms was conducted so that staff could witness the impact of the lessons on their students. Rather than relying on staged instructional videos, the Atlantic City Board of Education staff members wanted to see how their students would respond to these model literacy lessons based on their current reading levels and prior knowledge with the content. Staff were also given the option to participate in an online lesson planning course based on the prerequisites of the literacy lesson so as to begin building their own portfolio of engaging lessons.

SUMMARY

This chapter presented an innocent make-shift probe embedding critical math concepts that upon closer scrutiny revealed fundamental pedagogical misconceptions about the manner in which many students are expected to learn new concepts and processes. Students do not learn in isolation, they require real-world connections, both internal and external, to grasp and apply new concepts and skills within an authentic context.

The use of 21st Century Themes as articulated by the Partnership for the 21st Century Skills provides a clearly defined set of themes in which classroom teachers can build dynamic learning experiences that promote high levels of H.E.A.T.® in the classroom and elevate student achievement. Each theme provides an authentic context to promote connections, collaboration, and real-world problem solving.

Naysayers, however, may point to the significant time required to design student-learning experiences that target authentic connections; however, one must weigh the initial time investment against the months and years of frustration because students are unable to recognize the main idea in a reading passage or convert fractions to decimals in a high school algebra class, even though they have been exposed to these concepts and skills for many years.

Similar to asking classroom teachers to make internal connections among concepts, instructional leaders need to make internal connections between Digital Age Best Practices and different instructional priorities ranging from increasing student achievement to new teacher evaluation systems. As we explore Chapter 4 and its focus on the Digital Age Best Practice *Accelerating individual growth through vertical/horizontal differentiation*, consider the following questions meta-cognitive:

- What are simple ways of promoting both vertical and horizontal differentiated instruction in literacy and math classrooms?
- How prevalent are the practices of differentiated instruction on your campus?
- Does differentiated instruction require differentiated leadership?

4

Accelerating Individual Growth Through Vertical and Horizontal Differentiation

As mentioned in a previous chapter, differentiated instruction is an instructional strategy that maximizes learning for all students—regardless of skill level, interests, or background. In a typical classroom, students vary in their academic readiness, learning styles, modality strengths, interests, and prior knowledge levels. When a teacher differentiates instruction, he or she uses the optimum teaching practices and strategies to create different pathways for diverse learners to achieve the same academic standards.

Let's clarify horizontal versus vertical differentiation. Horizontal differentiation represents adjustments to the learning episode (i.e., content, process, product) based on student interests (e.g., sports, music, hobbies) and/or dominant learning modalities (e.g., visual learners, learners with a strong musical intelligence, concrete sequential learners). Vertical differentiation involves adjustments to the learning episode based on the ability or academic readiness level of the student. As a Digital Age Best Practice, both horizontal and vertical differentiated instruction have many advantages over traditional didactic instruction:

- Meet the needs of diverse students with a variety of learning styles and interests
- Provide learning opportunities for all students with different learning experiences
- Stimulate creativity and enable students to achieve a higher level of cognitive processing
- Promote the use of assessment as a vehicle to drive instructional decision making
- Support the tenets of student-centered learning in the classroom

Horizontal and vertical differentiated instruction manifest differently based on individual and group student profiles. Consider the following scenarios outlining a lesson plan and a unique student profile in Figures 4.0 and 4.1.

Figure 4.0   Scenario: Propaganda Techniques

Grade Level: High School

Topic: Propaganda Techniques

Scenario: The word *propaganda* refers to any technique that attempts to influence the opinions, emotions, attitudes, or behavior of a group, *in order to benefit the sponsor*. The purpose of propaganda is to *persuade*.

Prior Learning: Students have already demonstrated competency earlier through activities that addressed and assessed their understanding of the concept of propaganda.

Step 1: Brainstorm different propaganda techniques used in advertising versus politics.

Step 2: Select a topic, issue, or theme that can serve as the basis for a persuasive essay.

Step 3: Select Persuasion Map from the student materials section of the Read•Write•Think website (www.readwritethink.org).

(Continued)

Figure 4.0 (Continued)

Step 4: Complete your persuasion map for the topic, issue, or theme under consideration.

Performance Task: Students will create a persuasive ad campaign for a hypothetical product whose target audience is high school students.

Student Profile: Readiness
   Sid Youngblood is a very bright but academically unmotivated and unchallenged student. To him, the best class is the one that is "over." He seems to glide through school maintaining a B average while waiting for baseball practice to start. If baseball did not exist at school, chances are that Sid would probably be in an alternative school setting. He dislikes lectures and teachers constantly talking.

Student Profile: Interests
   Sid is interest in baseball, getting drafted, and becoming a major league shortstop. He also loves to fish and party with his friends.

Student Profile: Learning Profile
   Sid is definitely an interpersonal learner and loves to be the center of attention. He will do most anything to please his friends. He is also very tactile, kinesthetic.

Differentiated Instruction: How would you differentiate the performance task for the Propaganda Techniques lesson for a male eleventh-grade student, Sid Youngblood, who possesses the student profile above?
   Based on Sid's profile, it would make sense to involve him in some type of flexible grouping that would enable him to flourish in a group configuration. Given that students have the option to select a product for a persuasive ad campaign, it would be of little surprise that his product choice would be athletic equipment or apparel. Involving Sid in some type of video commercial where he would have to demonstrate the product would further align to his learning profile addressing tactile, kinesthetic learners.

Figure 4.1   Scenario: Online Survey

Grade Level: Intermediate

Topic: Online Survey

Scenario: You will design an online survey to collect data from a designated sampling of individuals regarding a controversial issue at home, at school, or in the community.

Prior Learning: Students have already demonstrated competency earlier through activities that addressed and assessed their understanding of opinion surveys.

Step 1: Decide on a topic or issue in which you would like to collect data.

Step 2: Follow the procedures from the New Survey category to design your new survey.

Step 3: After designing your new survey, choose Collect to create a link for an email message.

Step 4: Open a new window and go to the designated URL to complete your survey.

Step 5: Choose Analyze to view a graphic representation of your data collection.

Student Profile: Readiness

Melissa scored as a gifted and talented student but barely maintains a C average. Her grades are either As or incompletes. She is an exceptional young writer, especially fiction, but tends to write in an unconventional way. She is extremely curious and always needs to find connections between one subject and another. Melissa asks lots of questions.

Student Profile: Interests

She tends to shy away from anything related to mathematics or anything else that she does not think she is good at. She loves reading stories from dawn to dusk.

Student Profile: Learning Profile

Melissa needs discussion and is very auditory. A teacher better know her stuff, or Melissa will identify and draw attention to her deficiencies. Parents expect a certain level of performance, so Melissa does the minimum amount of schoolwork to maintain her active social life with her friends. However, if she is interested in a topic, she will go to any length to excel. Without praise, she quits. She is definitely a teacher pleaser.

Differentiated Instruction: How would you differentiate the performance task for the Propaganda Techniques lesson for a female fifth-grade student, Melissa Allen, who possesses the student profile above?

Based on Melissa's profile, it might be optimal to let her self-select a controversial issue within her local community as the focal point for the online survey. This approach will ensure her "buy-in" to this learning experience, which is part of a larger learning contract. Providing her with additional options relating to the final product as well as opportunities for self-assessment and peer review will increase opportunities for praise—a nonnegotiable item based upon her learning profile.

The two scenarios illustrate how careful blending of vertical and horizontal differentiated instructional strategies can elevate student engagement and performance in the classroom. A short summary of additional differentiated instructional strategies follows:

Anchor Activities. Teachers design ongoing activities directly related to the curriculum that individuals or pairs of students work on independently. Anchor activities represent logical extensions of learning during an instructional unit, offering meaningful work for students who either need more challenging tasks (e.g., when they finish early) or who are not engaged in classroom activities (e.g., compliant).

Compacted Curriculum. Teachers identify learning objectives, pre-testing students for prior mastery of these concepts, skills, and processes, and eliminate needless teaching practice and instructional activities if mastery can be documented. Compacting the curriculum helps to streamline the learning process, providing students with a challenging learning environment void of previously mastered material.

Flexible Grouping. Teachers consider the needs of both individuals and the group. Teachers choose a grouping strategy that is appropriate to the lesson and facilitates optimum learning. Teachers organize students into various grouping patterns (e.g., whole class, large group, small groups, triads, pairs, individualized instruction). Flexible grouping allows the teacher to instruct students on the basis of learning needs and allows the students to experience the value of collaboration.

Learning Centers/Stations. Learning centers, also referred to as learning stations, are areas set up around the classroom that are designed for a specific activity. At the different centers, students focus on developing and/or mastering a particular skill and/or concept while working either individually or in groups.

Learning Contract. Learning contracts are agreements between a teacher and a learner (or occasionally a group of learners). They normally concern issues of assessment and provide a viable mechanism for reassuring both parties about whether a planned work sample will meet the requirements of an instructional unit; however, learning contracts may also outline other criteria, including expectations, roles, and responsibilities for a given learning experience.

Personal Agendas. Personal agendas provide students with an individualized list of projects or activities to complete based on the student's interests or readiness level.

Tiered Instruction. Tiered instruction is a means of teaching one concept and meeting the different learning needs in a group. Teachers use varied levels of tasks to ensure that students explore ideas and use skills at a level that builds on what they already know and encourages growth. While students work at varied degrees of difficulty on their assigned tasks, they all explore the same essential ideas aligned to the same academic standards but work at different levels of cognitive processing.

Practical Application

The use of the Digital Age Best Practice *Accelerating individual growth through vertical/horizontal differentiation* enabled Atlantic City Board of Education staff to recognize how differentiating the content, process, and/or product based on learner readiness, interest, and learning profiles produced better results in terms of student comprehension of the critical math and literacy content.

In an elementary math classroom, the primary teacher implemented a three-station rotation involving tiered instruction with the aid of the classroom inclusion and resource teachers. One group of students was using a set of base ten blocks to explore fractions. A second group was completing the designated math skill builder that focused on converting fractions to decimals, while a third group of students participated in a mini-lesson addressing strategies for simplifying or reducing fractions.

In a middle school math classroom, the teacher organized a "speed" station approach involving a set of seven math stations. Each group of students (three or four students) was presented with a learning station card (see Figure 4.2) that contained a specific task that needed to be completed within a five- to seven-minute time period. As the students completed the task, an online timer that was expanded to cover the entire interactive whiteboard screen counted down the time to zero. Once the timer expired, students were given thirty seconds to rotate to the next math station.

The set of seven math stations always included a minimum of one station devoted to (a) student tactile/kinesthetic modality strengths (e.g., measuring the classroom dimensions to determine

Figure 4.2   Circle Grid II Station

Circle Grid II

Station 5:
Big Ideas: Radius, Diameter, Circumference, Area

Materials:
Pencil and paper

Purpose: Students work in a small group to determine the radius, diameter, area, and circumference of circles.

Instructions:

Step 1: What is the radius and circumference of the circle?

Step 2: If the circumference was 25% larger, what would be the new radius?

Step 3: Use the Student Answer Sheet to record your responses.

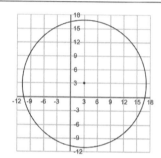

the circumference of the largest circle to fit inside the classroom), (b) real-world problem solving (e.g., determining the circular diameter of floodlights needed to highlight the dancers in a *Dancing With the Stars* episode), (c) some type of online quiz to assess student comprehension and application of pertinent concepts, and (d) a teacher-generated problem that modeled one of the math skill builders.

In an elementary literacy classroom, the use of differentiated strategies, including flexible grouping, tiered instruction, and learning station, reflect the district's literacy collaborative project. The guided reading component enables students to engage in different reading genres based on their reading level and interests. The use of flexible grouping occurs on a daily basis as students participate in both small group and large group instruction based on reading level and personal preferences.

Implementation Challenges

As with other Digital Age Best Practices, issues relating to time were a central concern to all teachers. How do I manage to fit everything

I am expected to teach while attempting to differentiate instruction? And how can I differentiate instruction while implementing the 5E Model? These were questions often raised by teachers during job-embedded modeling sessions, formal workshops, and summer institutes.

In-Class Modeling

Job-embedded modeling provided opportunities for teachers to gauge how much their classroom routines would be altered by employing differentiated strategies to their repertoire of instructional strategies. Teachers were encouraged to actively participate in the modeling sessions as a way of increasing their confidence level and developing a level of esprit de corp with district trainers.

Summer Institutes

The math summer institutes enabled teachers to participate as students in mock 5E math lessons that integrated the use of learning stations. Fortunately, the 5E Model provides sufficient flexibility in which to integrate learning stations into the very fabric of the learning experience. The five stages comprising the 5E Model include opportunities for both teacher-directed and student-directed learning. Specific learning stations were inserted in stages of the model normally reserved for student-directed activities, so as to minimize the impact on a teacher's "rhythm of instruction" and concern that students might miss some of their instruction if separated from the rest of the class.

SUMMARY

This chapter explored the benefits of the Digital Age Best Practice *Accelerating individual growth through vertical/horizontal differentiation.* Given the frequency and variety of both formal and informal assessments conducted in classrooms nationwide, ranging from benchmark assessments to informal reading inventories, the need to differentiate or adjust classroom instruction is now a requirement rather than a recommendation. Today's digital age learners are not necessarily different than previous generations in terms of their modality strengths, dominant intelligences, or preferences for real-world connections (contrary to the theory espoused in *Digital Natives, Digital Immigrants*), but, the fact that they have been tested, poked, and observed more so than any of their predecessors makes them a generation of learners demanding a differentiated approach in the classroom.

As we explore Chapter 5 and its focus on the Digital Age Best Practice *Anchoring student learning with digital age tools and resources,* consider the following questions:

- How can digital tools and resources best impact student achievement in the classroom?
- What are the best uses of digital tools and resources in differentiated classrooms?
- How can instructional leaders leverage their existing digital infrastructure to have the greatest impact on instruction and assessment?

5

Anchoring Student Learning With Digital Age Tools and Resources

Charles Dickens's classic *A Tale of Two Cities* easily applies to classroom use of digital tools and resources and their subsequent impact on teaching and learning. Consider the following: two sixth-grade science classrooms each possess an interactive board and a class set of computers (e.g., laptops, mobile devices). In Classroom A, the teacher uses the interactive board for large group instruction on earth systems, specifically the impact of greenhouse gases on the environment. Students use class computers to gather information on topics related to greenhouse gases (e.g., carbon cycle, ocean levels, fossil fuels) and later to create presentations showcasing the content as a PowerPoint presentation or for the more technical students, some form of movie, slideshow, and/or webpage.

In Classroom B, digital access is the same as Classroom A, but the teacher and students use them differently. Students view a You-Tube video on two different perspectives on the greenhouse gas argument and then work in teams to arrive at their own conclusions and generate practical solutions (if needed, based on their findings) that they can implement at home, school, or within their community to mitigate the problem (e.g., reducing one's carbon footprint). Students are presented with options throughout the lesson sequence including (a) self-selecting different primary and secondary source documents and resources (e.g., videoconference from a local environmental chemist) to gather information about the problem, (b) contacting key individuals in their community using different Web 2.0 tools (e.g., Google Apps) to get feedback about their conclusions, and (c) outlining a viable course of action using a concept mapping application such as Inspiration.

A quick H.E.A.T. analysis of the outcomes from Classrooms A and B in Figures 5.0 and 5.1 reveal two different H.E.A.T. (Higher-Order Thinking, Engaged Learning, Authentic Connections, Technology Use) profiles pertaining to student learning. The reader will quickly note the major difference in the two classrooms was not the technology but the instructional choices made by the two teachers relating to the use of the digital resources.

Figure 5.0   Classroom A: H.E.A.T. Lesson Plan Scoring Guide

Higher-Order Thinking

1. Students take notes only, do not ask questions.

2. Students learn/question at remembering level.

3. *Students learn/question at understanding level.*

4. Students learn/question at applying level.

5. Students learn/question at analyzing level.

6. Students learn/question at evaluating/creating levels.

Engaged Learning

1. *Students report what they have learned only.*

2. Students collaborate what they have learned with possible options.

3. Students solve a teacher-directed problem.

4. Students collaborate to solve a teacher-directed problem with possible options.

5. Students collaborate to define the task, the process, and/or the solution.

6. Students collaborate to define the task, the process, and/or the solution; collaboration extends beyond the classroom.

Authentic Connections

1. The learning experience is missing or too vague to determine relevance.

2. ***The learning experience provides no real-world application or represents a group of connected activities.***

3. The learning experience provides limited real-world relevance.

4. The learning experience provides extensive real-world relevance, but does not apply the learning to a real-world situation.

5. The learning experience provides real-world relevance and opportunity for students to apply their learning to a real-world situation.

6. The learning experience is directly relevant to students and involves creating a product that has a purpose beyond the classroom that directly impacts the students.

Technology Use

1. Digital tools and/or environmental resources are (1) not available, (2) not used, or (3) not directly connected to the learning.

2. Students' use of digital tools and/or environmental resources appears to be an add-on or is not needed for task completion.

3. Teacher leads whole-group learning with digital tools and/or environmental resources.

4. ***Students use teacher-directed digital tools and/or environmental resources to accomplish learning outcomes.***

5. Students use self-selected digital tools and/or environmental resources to accomplish learning outcomes.

6. Students use self-selected digital resources to accomplish learning outcomes beyond conventional strategies.

Today, there is a seemingly endless array of online resources at the proverbial fingertips of most teachers and students. Knowing when and where to use them is the secret. Leveraging digital tools and resources to elevate student achievement, ranging from a single computer in the classroom to one-to-*x* mobile device initiatives, is not a luxury but a necessity. In year's past, some of my colleagues have suggested that some educators still feel uncomfortable or intimidated

Figure 5.1   Classroom B: H.E.A.T. Lesson Plan Scoring Guide

Higher-Order Thinking

1. Students take notes only; do not ask questions.

2. Students learn/question at remembering level.

3. Students learn/question at understanding level.

4. Students learn/question at applying level.

5. Students learn/question at analyzing level.

6. ***Students learn/question at evaluating/creating levels.***

Engaged Learning

1. Students report what they have learned only.

2. Students collaborate to report what they have learned with possible options.

3. Students solve a teacher-directed problem.

4. Students collaborate to solve a teacher-directed problem with possible options.

5. Students help define the task, the process, and/or the solution.

6. ***Students help define the task, the process, and/or the solution; collaboration extends beyond the classroom.***

Authentic Connection

1. The learning experience is missing or too vague to determine relevance.

2. The learning experience provides no real-world application or represents a group of connected activities.

3. The learning experience provides limited real-world relevance.

4. The learning experience provides extensive real-world relevance, but does not apply the learning to a real-world situation.

5. ***The learning experience provides real-world relevance and opportunity for students to apply their learning to a real-world situation.***

6. The learning experience is directly relevant to students and involves creating a product that has a purpose beyond the classroom that directly impacts the students.

Technology Use

1. Digital tools and/or environmental resources are (1) not available, (2) not used, or (3) not directly connected to the learning.

2. Students' use of digital tools and/or environmental resources appears to be an add-on or is not needed for task completion.

3. Teacher leads whole group learning with digital tools and/or environmental resources.

4. Students use teacher-directed digital tools and/or environmental resources to accomplish learning outcomes.

5. ***Students use self-selected digital tools and/or environmental resources to accomplish learning outcomes.***

6. Students use self-selected digital resources to accomplish learning outcomes beyond conventional strategies.

---

with using technology in the classroom. My contention is that the issue is not so much using technology in the classroom but using technology effectively.

Practical Application

Leveraging the existing digital tools in the Atlantic City School District and supporting the Digital Age Best Practice *Anchor student learning with digital age tools and resources* required that the district first consider which digital tools would deliver the biggest return on investment in terms of impacting teaching and learning. The district focused on providing classrooms with a basic set of digital tools, including flexible interactive boards, document cameras, computer work stations, and access to laptop/iPad carts. Given the sheer number of available Web 2.0 apps, the literacy and math lesson plans developed in house focused on a core group of applications that provided the necessary flexibility to be incorporated into any large group, small group, or individualized student work environment. These apps also offered classrooms the fastest and easiest way to impact their instructional curriculum, promote high levels of H.E.A.T. in student learning, and elevate student engagement. Given the rapid rise and fall of new applications (also known as apps), I organized these apps by category rather than by the specific name of the resource.

Web 2.0 Spreadsheet Applications

Web-based spreadsheets, such as Edit Grid or Google Apps, provide a transparent outlet for students to work collaboratively as they gather, organize, display, and analyze data. Edit Grid enables students to enter data into the same spreadsheet remotely from multiple locations, which promotes expanded sampling, shared data analysis, and collaborative decision making. Figure 5.2 provides a sample Web 2.0 spreadsheet (e.g., Edit Grid) that was used to collect student data from a middle school math investigation in the Atlantic City School District addressing the Common Core State Standards relating to measures of central tendency and variability. In this experiment, students were determining their reaction time using the simulation Online Reaction Time Test (www.getyourwebsitehere.com/jswb/rttest01.html) to determine which sex (men or women) has the fastest reaction time.

Figure 5.2   Edit Grid

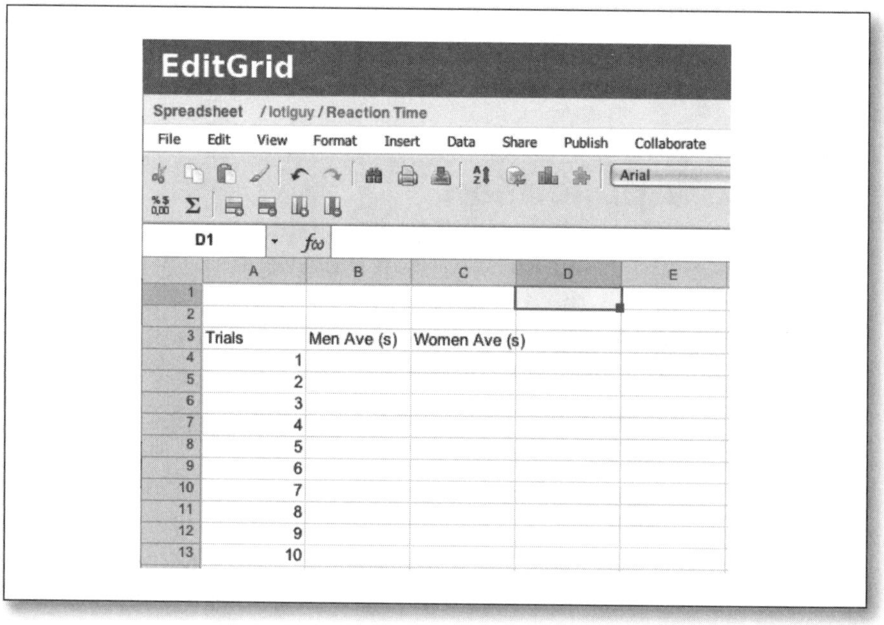

Word Clouds

Word clouds were integrated throughout the district's Grade 5 through 8 literacy investigations as a pre-reading activity to encourage student analysis skills, develop vocabulary, and promote student interest in each reading selection. Word clouds are online applications that transform standard text into a text cloud where the size of the word is based on how frequently it is used in the text passage.

Figure 5.3 Inaugural Speech (Kennedy, 1961)

Source: www.wordle.net

Figure 5.4 Inaugural Speech (Obama, 2009)

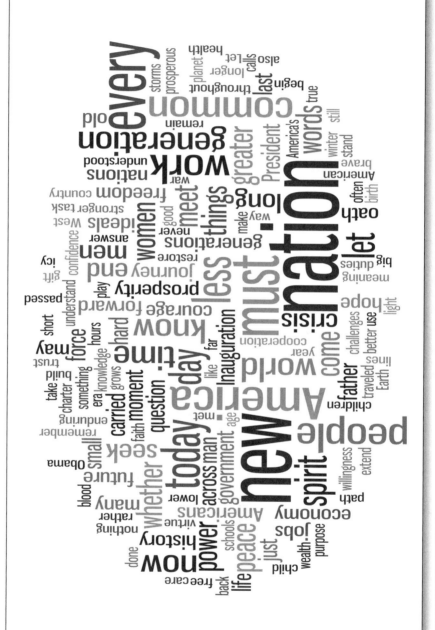

Source: www.wordle.net

Popular word cloud apps, such as Wordle and TagCrowd, enable staff at all levels to broaden student text-to-text and text-to-world connections as well as serve as an informal assessment strategy to determine student prior knowledge. Figures 5.3 and 5.4 provide two word cloud illustrations used in a high school government class to ascertain student prior knowledge about U.S. presidents and the issues confronting their administrations. The students were asked which word cloud, Figure 5.3 or Figure 5.4, represents the inaugural address of President Kennedy in 1961 or President Obama in 2009.

Web-Based Videos

Web-based videos, including the Kahn Academy series of videos and YouTube, were seamlessly integrated into the district's literacy and math initiative using the district-adopted 5E lesson plan model. I mentioned specifically the 5E Model because selected YouTube video clips were used extensively in the Engagement section of the model to generate student interest in a particular topic as well as create a level of student dissonance relating to the topic based on the selected video. Figure 5.5 displays a screenshot from the YouTube video clip *The Most Shocking Video of the Tsunami,* which was used as

Figure 5.5   Tsunami

Source: Wikimedia Commons

a free writing activity in the Engagement section of a literacy investigation on earthquakes.

Figure 5.6 displays a screenshot from the Kahn Academy focusing on ratios and proportions that provided an easy fit into the district-adopted 5E Model section called Explanation. By the way, the Kahn Academy website was also one of the early pioneers of the concept of the flipped classroom—a philosophy that promotes student exposure to new and existing content away from the classroom (i.e., as homework), thus promoting more application and hands-on inquiry relating to the actual content in the classroom.

Figure 5.6   Khan Academy

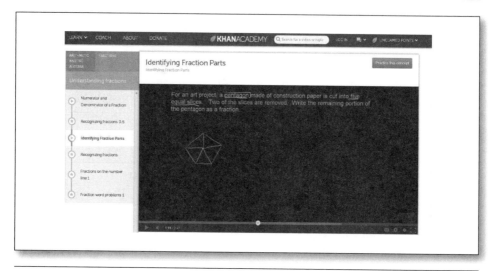

Source: All Khan Academy content is available for free at www.khanacademy.org.

Online Simulations

One of the most under-utilized web-based applications is the use of online simulations to elevate student H.E.A.T. levels in the classroom. These simulations range in sophistication from an interactive social studies applet called 270towin (see Figure 5.7) to a reaction time simulation used in a math classroom to reinforce student application of central tendency. The 270towin website (www.270towin.com) enables students to work as presidential campaign strategists as they attempt to flip targeted states for the upcoming election. Though some of these online simulations appear on the surface as an online game, their ability to motivate students, help contextualize math and literacy concepts, and make real-world connections cannot be ignored.

Figure 5.7   270towin

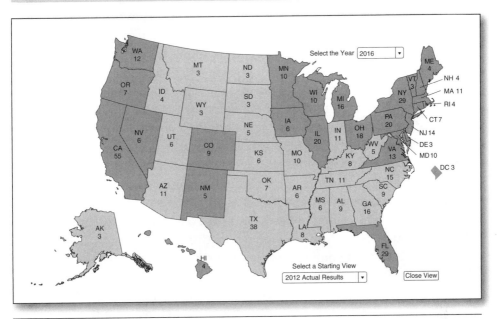

Source: 2016 Presidential Election Interactive Map and History of the Electoral College, www.270towin.com

Content Management Systems

Content-management systems range from the simple TinyURL to a course management system, such as Blackboard, Moodle, and WebXT. The systems, depending on their level of sophistication, also provide teachers and students with easy access to web links, threaded and non-threaded discussions, and uploading capabilities. The more advanced systems also provide a painless mechanism to create online quizzes, record grades, and build online courses. In the Atlantic City School District, the technology division acquired a Moodle server for staff to create their own blended learning environments and participate in district-approved online professional development courses.

Implementation Challenges

The major challenge for executing the Digital Age Best Practice *Anchoring student learning with digital age tools and resources* was the age of many of the existing school buildings. Prior to the construction of two new campuses, Pennsylvania Avenue School and Richmond Avenue School in the Atlantic City School District, three of the campuses were already over ninety years old. Providing adequate wireless Internet connections in some classrooms, let alone finding sufficient electrical power for the computers, has provided a formidable challenge. The district's commitment to a viable digital infrastructure was evident most prominently in the amount of teacher support offered throughout the school system.

Each campus has a full-time technology coordinator whose primary responsibility is to support and promote high levels of H.E.A.R.T. in the classroom. The technology coordinators work with individual campus' PLCs (professional learning community) and/or grade-level teams offering a broad array of support services ranging from facilitating online courses on engaged learning to conducting small group instruction on the use of digital cameras in the classroom. The strategic move made by the Atlantic City Board of Education was ensuring a high level of accountability for the performance level of each of the campus technology coordinators. The district supervisor of technology is directly involved in the evaluation of each of the campus technology coordinators to ensure that expectations relating to H.E.A.R.T. are clearly communicated and modeled systemwide. The results of their implementation efforts produced significant gains in each of the categories comprising H.E.A.R.T.

SUMMARY

This chapter used Charles Dickens's classic *Tale of Two Cities* to illustrate that, given similar digital infrastructures, two classrooms can have marked differences in their actual technology implementation practices depending on the skill of the technology coordinators and the expectations of campus and district leadership. Balancing the three elements embedded in any successful technology integration effort (hardware, support, leadership) are pivotal to maximizing the technology investment and its alignment with curricular priority areas.

Unfortunately, examples abound where dynamic uses of digital tools have both showcased and augmented authentic learning episodes in the classroom yet have been overshadowed by statewide test scores that have either remained stagnant or decreased when compared to the state averages. In Chapter 6, we will explore how the Digital Age Best Practice *Clarifying student understanding with formative assessments* can augment digital tool use as well as the other best practices by ensuring that student feedback is used to drive the instructional process using both formal and informal formative assessments. As you read Chapter 6, consider the following questions:

- How effective is your content benchmarking process for achieving results on statewide assessments?
- What informal assessment strategies beyond "Are there any questions?" have you integrated into your classroom or campus assessment plan?
- How can the strategic use of formative assessments elevate student achievement in the classroom?

6

Clarifying Student Understanding With Formative Assessments

In Herbert Kohl's book *I Won't Learn From You—and Other Thoughts on Creative Maladjustments*, the author discusses the personal phenomenon of the "not-learning" mode. According to Kohl, when students decide, "I won't learn from you," they go into not-learning mode. Not-learning describes any number of behaviors that a learner uses to keep new information from getting into the brain. With younger children, the not-learning mode may manifest as students putting their hands over their ears; however, with adolescents and older teenagers, the not-learning mode becomes more passive and takes the form of silent monologues, staring, or in some instances, FOD (face on desk).

When the proverbial "Are there any questions?" is asked by the classroom teacher, how many students raise their hand and articulate a viable question relating to the topic, and, in contrast, how many students carry on a silent monologue in their head? One could argue that asking, "Are there any questions?" is more of a reminder to students that class is about to end rather than an opportunity to delve deeper into the content under investigation.

The same futility can also be applied to more formative assessment schemes commonly referred to as benchmark testing. One major issue with formative assessments is the over-testing syndrome manifested in weekly chapter tests, combinations of teacher-made and standardized criterion-referenced tests, frequent concept-specific and tutorial-based (e.g., fractions, decimals, percentages) online tests, and annual norm-referenced tests.

Based on the above examples, one can conclude that the art of testing based on the sheer volume of tests administered has been mastered, yet in most instances, the science of analyzing the data, formulating hypotheses about which interventions to choose from, assessing the merits of the follow-up interventions for addressing student content/skill deficiencies has not. In this chapter, we will address strategies to bolster the formative assessment process, both informal and formal, as well as address some of the implementation hurdles associated with its practice.

Practical Application

The use of the Digital Age Best Practice *Clarifying student understanding with formative assessments* provides the best medium for assessing student progress. Informal assessments allow teachers to track the ongoing progress of their students regularly and often. These assessments are designed to determine whether students are learning what is being taught, for the purpose of adjusting instruction. By using informal assessments, teachers can target students' specific problem areas, adapt instruction, and intervene earlier rather than later. In Figure 6.0 is a description of an A–Z list of informal assessment techniques that can readily augment or replace the "Are there any questions?" approach.

In short, informal assessment strategies, a branch of the formative assessment model, can provide teachers with instantaneous data in which to make daily data-driven adjustments to their operational curriculum impacting individual students. Formal assessment practices, most notably benchmark testing, when implemented systematically, can answer the question "Are students really learning anything in my classroom?" over an extended period of time.

Benchmark testing is not a new instructional concept. As mentioned earlier, the low fidelity of its implementation has given the

Figure 6.0   A–Z List of Informal Assessment Techniques

anecdotal records. Anecdotal records represent informal written descriptions of a student's academic progress in the classroom involving a specific problem or area of difficulty. The record is a result of a direct observation. Anecdotal records can be used to document student achievement within any content area. Be careful—anecdotal records should be written carefully, avoiding judgmental words.

blog. A blog is short for weblog and represents an online journal that is frequently updated by the students based on the current content or problem under investigation. Blogs are typically updated daily and require little or no technical background to update and maintain. Blogs can be used by students to create their own online content journal.

brainstorming. Brainstorming is a technique used to determine what a student may already know about a particular topic. Students often feel free to participate because there is no criticism or judgment.

chain notes. Students pass around an envelope on which the teacher has written one question about the class. When the envelope reaches a student, he or she takes a moment to respond to the question and then places the response in the envelope.

checklists. Checklists (e.g., misconception/preconception checklist) specify student behavior/products expected during daily progression through the curriculum. The items on the checklist may be behavior or content area objectives. A checklist is considered to be a type of observational technique. Because observers check only the presence or absence of the product or behavior, checklists generally are reliable and relatively easy to use. Used over time, checklists can document students' rate and degree of accomplishment within the curriculum.

debates. Debates enable the teacher to informally evaluate students' oral work by assessing their oral presentation skills in terms of their ability to understand concepts and present them to others in an orderly fashion.

directed paraphrasing. Ask students to write a layman's "translation" of something they have just learned—geared to a specified individual or audience—to assess their ability to comprehend and transfer concepts.

exit cards. Exit cards are a quick assessment tool for teachers to help them become more aware of student understanding of concepts taught. Exit cards are written student responses to questions posed at the end of a class or learning activity or at the end of a day. They may be used at any grade level and every subject area.

follow-up questioning. Quality follow-up questions generated by either a teacher or student from an observation, comment, or prior question extend beyond simple rote memorization, such as *What is . . . ?* or *Where did . . . ?* by encompassing the higher levels of Bloom's Taxonomy.

gallery walk.   In small groups, students move around the room from station to station at set times and discuss questions or problems raised during class. For example, a math teacher could post three to five questions about a particular math problem on separate sheets of paper taped as stations on the wall. Groups of students would pause at each station, discuss the question, write comments on the sheet, and then go to the next question when a signal is given.

graphic organizers. Graphic organizers or concept maps provide students with a visual representation that supports their understanding of simple or complex processes. Sample graphic organizers include T-charts, Venn diagrams, and KWL charts. Graphic organizers can be used to assess students' understanding of relationships, ideas, or concepts.

guided reciprocal peer questioning. Guided reciprocal peer questioning enables students to develop questions about new material or recognize what they don't know. Students are given open-ended questions (e.g., Explain how . . . , What if . . . ? How does _____ affect _____?) that they ask each other.

hand signals.   Hand signals range from students raising their hands to respond to a question posed by the teacher to a group "thumbs up/down" signal to determine students' "acknowledged" understanding of a concept or process.

interviews. Perform either a structured or unstructured interview with one or more students to ascertain their understanding of a particular concept or process.

journals—learning/reflection. Reflection or learning journals enable students to reflect on the learning going on within the classroom. Daily journals provide students with a daily conversation with themselves, allowing them to reflect on key concepts or ideas raised during class.

KWL chart. A KWL (know, want, learn) chart is a graphic organizer that allows students to determine what they *know* about a specific topic, what they *want to know/learn* about a specific topic, and what they *learned* from the lesson. These charts are used to gauge students' understanding of a particular concept or process.

learning logs. Learning logs provide opportunities to gauge student progress. A learning log is a student's ongoing commentary about a particular course of study. Entries are made frequently and are dated.

(Continued)

Figure 6.0 (Continued)

minute paper. The minute paper is an informal assessment technique that asks students a simple question about some aspect of the class that they can answer in a minute. The responses are then collected by the teacher on three-by-five cards, reviewed, and distributed back to the students with comments or other interesting points.

muddiest point. The muddiest point is an informal assessment strategy used to help the teacher identify a lesson's most confusing points. Students are asked to write down the most confusing or problematic concept from a given lesson via a three-by-five card or email message to the teacher. The teacher, in turn, collects the "muddiest points" from the students and then addresses these issues more completely during a follow-up lesson.

"no hands up." A "no hands up" rule gives the whole class thinking time to prepare a response before the teacher chooses a student. Another approach is allowing hands up only when a student has a question of his or her own.

one-sentence summary. This simple technique challenges students to answer the questions, Who does what to whom, when, where, how, and why? (represented by the letters WDWWWWHW) about a given topic and then to synthesize those answers into a simple, informative, grammatically correct, and long summary sentence.

open-ended questions. Open-ended questions resist a simple or single right answer; are deliberately thought-provoking, counterintuitive, and/or controversial; require students to draw on content knowledge and personal experience; and address the highest level of Bloom's Taxonomy (evaluating/creating).

pairs check. Pairs check is a technique in which teams of four work in pairs on a problem. One student works on the problem while a second student coaches, and then these students switch roles. In the next step, each pair checks their work by checking with the other pair.

performance task. A performance task is a learning event that allows for multiple solutions, relates to the student's prior knowledge, has personal meaning, and is challenging. Performance tasks are used to determine what students know and what they are able to do relating to the eligible content.

quick write. A quick write is an informal assessment tool requiring students to write for a short time (less than ten minutes), focusing on content and not grammar.

roving reporter. A roving reporter is a member of a team who roams around the room seeking ideas and help from other groups.

RSQC2 (recall, summarize, question, comment, and connect). RSQC2 is a classroom assessment technique in which students are asked to recall and review information presented in prior lessons. Students write down a few of the main points from a previous lesson (recall) and then bring those separate ideas together into a single summary statement (summarize). Students then generate one unanswered question (question) they have from the previous lesson. They then provide a connection from the concepts in that lesson to the overall goals for the course (connect). Student may also be asked to comment about their understanding of the concepts.

rubrics. A rubric provides written guidelines by which student work is assessed. Grading rubrics articulate clearly how student work is judged and give standards needed to achieve each grade. Rubrics are useful for both students (what is expected from them is clearly articulated) and staff (makes grading easier and less subjective).

short quizzes. Short quizzes are usually one to three questions and may take the form of short answer, multiple-choice, fill-in-the-blank, or open-ended. Short quizzes are used informally to gauge what students have learned about the content.

student-generated test questions. Student-generated test questions allow students to write test questions and model answers for specified topics in a format consistent with course exams. This approach gives students the opportunity to evaluate the course topics, reflect on what they understand, and determine good potential test items.

surveys/rating scales. Surveys and rating scales provide an easy-to-use format to acquire information about students' understanding of important content. Online surveys in particular give students an opportunity to express their understanding of a concept or process without any potential embarrassment. Results from students are tabulated online and aggregated into a class graph or data table.

think-pair-share. Think-pair-share involves students thinking about a question, pairing off and discussing the question with a classmate, and then sharing their answers with the whole class.

think-pair-square. Think-pair-square is the same as think-pair-share except that students share their answers with another pair.

traffic light cards. Every student has a red, yellow, and green card. If a student shows their yellow card, it means the teacher is going too fast. If they want to stop and ask a question, they show red. The teacher can then choose a child showing green or yellow to answer.

turn-to-your-neighbor. This is a very useful technique for any size class. With this approach, staff give their students a problem to work on

(Continued)

Figure 6.0 (Continued)

(e.g., figures or tables to interpret, a written question) and simply ask them to "turn to their neighbors" in the class and discuss the problem. Students should work in small groups of three to four.

umpire. Umpire is a technique whereby one student responds to a teacher question, then the teacher immediately looks down the row of chairs or tables and points to another student or group of students to determine if they agree with the initial student's response (e.g., Do you agree with Tim's definition of circumference?, Is his answer correct?, or What do you think?).

videos of student portfolio conferences. Using video to document student products is a convenient way to determine what students have accomplished and what they know relative to the content standards.

wikis. A wiki is a website or similar online resource that allows users to add and edit content collectively.

write before discussion. Write before discussion is an approach used to enhance a discussion with "low stakes" writing. Students are asked a question and given a few minutes to briefly write answers or comments. What they write is for their use only and not handed in to the teacher. Students need to understand why this is useful for the discussion and how it can help them write better (otherwise they may not take the exercise seriously).

X Games. X Games is a spin-off of the extreme sports version whereby students are given "extreme" math problems to solve working in teams of four. The games can be held quarterly and broken into seasons based on the current math benchmark.

Y graphic organizer. A Y graphic organizer is a three-part chart embedded in a pie chart. In other words, the pie chart is divided into three sections forming the letter Y. A student can use a Y chart to help organize what they know about a topic by writing and/or drawing what the topic looks like, feels like, and sounds like. The student must think about a topic with respect to three of their senses: sight, hearing, and touch.

Z chart. Z charts show student progress over time and can result in many different charts showing various viewpoints. A Z chart may reduce at least three different line charts into one simple line chart. When reviewing progress of their performance in class, students will want to look at the following:

- In the short term, I want to know, how did I do this month (and/or week, etc.)?
- In the longer term, the rate of academic growth or decline may be of significant interest.
- In the intermediate term, it is interesting to connect these two, to see how short-term achievement is building up to longer-term goals.

practice a dubious reputation. In Chapter 2, I referenced four essential ingredients to a quality benchmarking system: (1) possesses the look and feel of the actual statewide assessment, (2) measures what has already been taught, (3) ensures an efficient turn-around time for data analysis and summary, and (4) provides follow-up interventions for students at a LoTi 3+.

A quality benchmarking program provides students with the look and feel of the actual statewide assessment. Why? Test-taking strategies can help familiarize students with various testing aspects, such as time limit, format, terminology, deductive reasoning, and answer selection. According to Gulek (2003), "Research indicates that test anxiety may exert a debilitating effect on student performance"; therefore, anything that "[helps] students prepare ahead of time" can "[increase] student confidence" (p. 45). One need look no further than the Internet for literally hundreds of sample statewide assessments in mathematics, science, and language arts literacy (reading and writing) that can be easily retrofitted with test questions to give students the "look and feel" of the actual statewide assessment.

A quality benchmark testing program measures what has been taught using a Pretest/Posttest Model. Oftentimes, students are presented with a summative assessment that does measure what has been taught, but not necessarily what has been learned. Without pretesting, there is no way to gauge if students have progressed or perhaps regressed with their content understanding over time. Figure 6.1 provides a graphic illustration of the Pretest/Posttest Model.

The use of pre/post assessments to generate group mean scores, conduct item analyses, and compare individual student results is

Figure 6.1   Pretest/Posttest Model

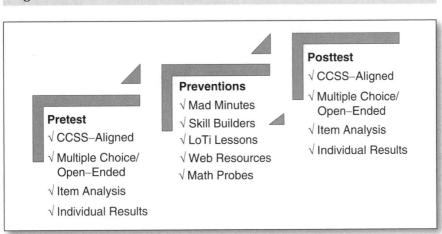

synonymous with most benchmarking protocols; what is unique in the Atlantic City Public Schools has been the role of the prevention section of the model. Identifying skills and concepts early on that students struggle with on the pretests affords staff members the opportunity to create and implement preventive measures (e.g., problems-of-the-day or skill builders, small group instruction) that address these areas of concern and, in many instances, prevent the reoccurrence of the same skill deficiency on the posttests.

The Pretest/Posttest Model provides concrete milestones for staff to organize their curriculum maps, scope and sequence charts, or unit plans. It also enables content and grade-level teams to create macro-plans for the next benchmark period based on the results of the current benchmark. Figure 6.2 illustrates a simple macro-plan based on the results of a pretest addressing the Common Core State Standards (CCSS) strand, geometry, involving Grades 6 and 7.

Figure 6.2   Macro-Plan: ABC School

ABC School

Cluster: Geometry

Based on the results of the benchmark pretest for geometry, it is recommended that

- Students use grade-appropriate rulers and formula/reference sheets based on CCSS guidelines as a component of daily instruction.
- The Grade 6 and 7 skill builders serve as the focus for math instruction and *not the textbook*. These skill builders address the fundamental skills that students need in the geometry cluster.
- The Grade 6 and 7 skill builders be arranged to fit each teacher's current scope and sequence/curriculum map for teaching in the geometry cluster.
- Staff become familiar with the test specifications based on the CCSS for their grade level as it relates to the math concepts in the geometry cluster (these skills are articulated below).

1. Theme: Plane Figures 2D

- Names and properties (Grade 6–7)
- Line and angles (Grade 6–7)
- Area of polygons (Grade 6–7)
- Area and circumference of a circle (Grade 7)
- Regular and irregular figures (Grade 6–7)

- Plotting plane figures on grids (Grade 6)
- Scale drawings of geometric shapes (Grade 7)

2. Theme: Solid Figures 3D

- Names and properties (Grade 6–7)
- Faces, vertices, and edges (Grade 6–7)
- Volume of right rectangular prism (Grade 6)
- Area, volume, and surface area (Grade 7)
- Represent three-dimensional figures using nets (Grade 6–7)

Providing students with a valid and reliable bank of test questions that match the format of the actual statewide assessment and evaluate the level of student growth in their understanding and application of the content are indicators of a strong benchmarking program. However, getting the benchmark results back to teachers in a timely fashion is critical. In the Atlantic City School District, the recommended protocol is a three-day turnaround between the submission of the benchmark assessments and the scanning and reporting of the data. Providing timely feedback gives teachers opportunity to adjust lesson episodes in response to areas of strengths and areas of deficiencies identified from the benchmark data.

Probably the most essential part of the benchmarking system is the recommended interventions (or preventions) that help to shape the teacher's instructional and operational curricula. As mentioned earlier, the intervention target is at a LoTi 3+. But that does not mean that all interventions need to be designed at this level. In mathematics, the use of daily skill builders or problems-of-the-day, mad minutes, and online resources provide students with foundational skill development that emphasizes repetition, contextualizing math concepts, and mathematical problem solving. Figure 6.3 provides a sample problem-of-the-day surrounding the math cluster geometry. In this sample problem-of-the-day, note how the math concepts of area and perimeter of polygons (rectangles and triangles) are contextualized within the broader concept, ratio.

Implementation Challenges

The importance of formative assessments, both informal and formal, in terms of promoting data-driven decision making cannot be overstated. Providing useful data impacting both short-term and

Figure 6.3   Skill Builder Grade 7, Problem 2

Math Problem of the Day

PROBLEM 2:

Ms. Martin is covering her patio with stone and grass.

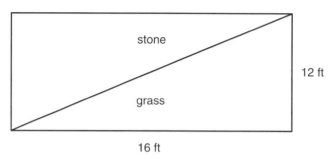

* What is the perimeter and area of the entire patio?

* What is the area of the section covered by stone?

* What is the ratio of the area of the section covered by stone to the area covered by grass?

long-term instructional decisions in the classroom and determining student growth in the learning process are two key attributes of the formative assessment process. Why then would there be any implementation challenges for executing a best practice that serves as one of the pillars for any K–16 curriculum model (i.e., evaluation)? In the Atlantic City School District as well as districts everywhere, this issue is not tied to the formative assessment process but to the change process.

The move to a formal benchmarking process in mathematics required staff members to change both what and how they were teaching. Given many teachers' reliance on their textbooks to drive math instruction, the change was, in many cases, drastic. What further complicated matters was the timing of the transition, because not only were teachers expected to move from a text-based approach for organizing their math curriculum to a benchmark-based process, but they also were in the process of moving from the current state standards to the CCSS. To address these issues, the district instituted a series of support measures to ensure a smooth transition throughout the entire process.

Summer Institutes

A four-day summer math institute was conducted for Grade 3 through 8 teachers over three consecutive summers. At these institutes, teachers rotated through a series of stations that ranged from increasing their understanding of the essential math concepts to using the benchmark topics to organize their operational curriculum. Separate break-out sessions addressed additional elements of the curriculum, including grouping configurations (differentiated instruction), developing lesson plans using the 5E Model, and locating the necessary instructional resources to support this transition. The institutes were facilitated by the district math coaches, the supervisor of math and science, district technology coordinators, and independent consultants.

In-Class Modeling

The role of in-class or job-embedded modeling continually serves as a cornerstone to the transition process to ensure that a high fidelity of implementation relating to the benchmarking methodology is present in all Grade 3 through 8 classrooms. Job-embedded modeling is particularly pivotal in the inclusion classrooms, especially for modeling small group and differentiated instruction with two full-time staff members.

Math Coaches

The Atlantic City School Board of Education hired five math coaches targeting the Grade 3 through 8 classrooms throughout the district. Their charge was to provide assistance with weekly lesson plans, perform job-embedded modeling, offer informal and formal professional development, develop benchmark assessments and problems-of-the-day in coordination with the supervisor of mathematics and science, conduct classroom probing of student math skills, and design follow-up interventions based on the results of the pretest/posttest benchmarking cycle. Yet, the collective expertise of the math coaches had little impact until they were able to establish an ongoing positive relationship with staff at the targeted grade levels—a relationship that grew over time during the summer institutes and job-embedded modeling sessions.

Building Leadership

Though research has documented the critical role of building level leadership in the change process, sometimes the available channels to provide this support are either misinterpreted or misunderstood. Each month during districtwide administrator meetings in the Atlantic City School District, time was devoted specifically to sharing with all district supervisors and building administrators the results of the most recent benchmark assessments as well as articulating expectations during the current benchmarking period.

Since key look-fors relating to the math implementation were embedded in the district H.E.A.R.T. walkthrough form, it was essential that all building leaders understood the current benchmark period, the key math concepts comprising this benchmark, and the types of instructional delivery that should be used to address these math concepts. For example, conducting a classroom H.E.A.R.T. walkthrough during a whole group lesson focusing exclusively on adding fractions when the current benchmark was expressions and equations could prove counter-productive over time because this approach could (a) limit students' opportunity to contextualize the use of fractions within the current benchmark expressions and equations, (b) limit student exposure to all of the math concepts embedded in the expressions and equations strand, and (c) jeopardize their performance level on the upcoming Expressions and Equations Benchmark Posttest.

SUMMARY

This chapter addressed two important strands relating to the formative assessment process: informal assessment practices and benchmarking. Collectively, they provide purposeful data in which to drive daily instructional decision making that results in targeted and effective differentiated instruction impacting all learners. Unlike many of the other best practices, the Digital Age Best Practice *Clarifying student understanding with formative assessments* requires that stakeholders at the classroom, building, and district levels adhere to a process that requires both the courage and the commitment to overcome possible instructional inertia because, in some cases, the process demands that we do things differently. For some teachers who already implement a standards-based approach to their instructional curriculum, the change process may appear minimal; for others who have relied in the past on their own scope and sequence charts or the chapters in the textbook, the change process becomes more dramatic and deeply personal.

As with the other best practices, the role of leadership is paramount. As we explore Chapter 7 and its emphasis on the Digital Age Best Practice *Implementing student-centered learning environments* consider the following questions:

- How can classrooms implement a student-centered learning environment within a standards-based curriculum framework?
- How does a classroom transition into a student-centered learning environment?
- Is a student-centered learning environment always better than a teacher-directed learning environment?

7

Implementing Student-Centered Learning Environments

Probably the least understood of the Digital Age Best Practices surrounds the individual educator's perceptions as to what precisely qualifies as a student-centered learning environment. Does a student deciding what he or she wants to learn, how and when they will learn it, and how they will demonstrate their mastery of the concept constitute student-centered learning? What about a student who embraces his or her newfound opportunity to work in a collaborative group that requires all group members to reach a consensus on ways of solving a mathematical problem? Is that student centered?

For ease in defining a student-centered learning environment, let's assume that any learning episode can be divided into three domains: content, process, and product (see Figure 7.0).

The content represents what the student needs to learn or how the student will get access to the information. The process identifies activities in which the student engages in order to make sense of or

Figure 7.0 Content, Process, and Product

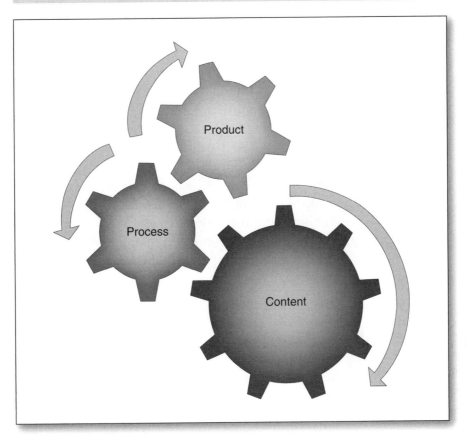

master the content. The product represents culminating projects that ask the student to rehearse, apply, and extend what he or she has learned in a unit or individual learning episode. In a typical classroom scenario, seldom are students vested with options, input, and/or decision-making involving all three domains. The Atlantic City Board of Education (ACBOE) defined a student-centered learning environment as one in which students were vested with options, input, and/or decision-making involving two out of three of these domains within any classroom learning episode.

For example, in a fourth-grade classroom the content may be defined by the teacher (e.g., New Jersey communities), but students are given options relating to the process (participate in a video-conference with the city manager to learn about the functions of city government, work in a small group using the Internet to learn about the functions of city government, complete an

I-Search paper on the functions of city government) as well as the final product (e.g., position paper about the role of city government, PowerPoint presentation, class debate). In a seventh-grade classroom, students might be given options relating to the math content (e.g., investigating ratio within the context of expressions and equations, geometry, or statistics and probability) and the final product (e.g., determining the amount of paint to cover the classroom walls, calculating the amount of fat in the main dish at a local restaurant, predicting the mean number of runs scored by the Yankees for the entire year based on their performance through the first 30 games), but the teacher defines the process (e.g., mathematical problem solving). In a high school literature classroom, students are given options relating to the content (e.g., informational text of their choice) and the process (e.g., choosing appropriate graphic organizers, looking for supportive evidence, analyzing word choice in the passage), but the teacher defines the final product (e.g., wiki entry).

Practical Application

There is no one magical formula for transitioning from a teacher-directed to a student-centered classroom. Oftentimes, variables relating to student readiness levels, interests, and learning profiles will dictate the number of options and input allowed by the teacher. Promoting "student-centeredness" in the classroom should start small and progress at a level commensurate with a student's ability to take ownership for their own learning. One of the easiest ways to start the process is by giving students choices relating to the process and product. Figure 7.1 provides a sample math menu for a group of seventh-grade students.

In the math menu, students are able to self-select the types of activities based on their level of complexity and real-world connection, yet they all address student application of algebraic equations. Besides an activity menu, other strategies for promoting student choices align with many of the differentiated instructional techniques outlined in Chapter 4 (e.g., anchor activities, personal agendas, learning contracts). As with differentiated instruction, the strategies you select to promote a student-centered classroom will be dependent on the readiness level of the students, their interests, and their learning profiles.

Figure 7.1   Solving Equations Activity Menu

Two Points

❏ Complete the Solving Equations Worksheet (Be sure to show all your work! No work = No credit).

❏ Play Solving Equations Millionaire Game online.

http://www.quia.com/rr/4096.html

❏ Create a cartoon depicting how to solve equations with all four operations with an example for each operation, either using paper and colored pencils or online.

http://www.makebeliefscomix.com/Comix

❏ Create a game (Jeopardy, Who Wants to Be a Millionaire, etc.) that a group of students could play to help review solving equations with all four operations for an upcoming test.

http://jeopardylabs.com

Five Points

❏ Create an equation to solve the following scenario: Anthony bought a new Audi automobile. The car gets 24 miles per gallon. He needs to travel 960 miles for work this month. How many gallons of gas will he use? Show your work or explain your answer. Afterwards, show what he will pay to fill up his car in three different cities nationally. You choose!

• United States Gas Price Heat Map

http://gasbuddy.com/gb_gastemperaturemap.aspx

❏ Same situation as above, but Anthony decides to purchase a 2012 Ferrari 612 Scaglietti that gets 16 miles per gallon. What will he pay for gas to travel from Carlsbad, California, to Roselle, New Jersey? Show your work or explain your answer.

• United States Gas Price Heat Map

http://gasbuddy.com/gb_gastemperaturemap.aspx

Ten Points (Individual or Group)

❏ Determine the heat loss of one of the hot water tanks at Grace Wilday Junior High School using the heat loss equation, and make recommendations either to maintain the current hot water tanks or replace them with a more energy efficient model. Show

(Continued)

SECTION II

A Converging Educational Landscape

School buildings nationwide have been on the receiving end of many initiatives targeting improved student achievement and teaching practices in the classroom. One of the most popular, the *Race to the Top* program sponsored and funded by the U.S. Department of Education, is one initiative that provides competitive funding to states that attempt to leverage existing resources with additional financial backing toward advancing reforms in four core areas: "(1) Adopting standards and assessments that prepare students to succeed in college and the workplace and to compete in the global economy; (2) Building data systems that measure student growth and success, and inform teachers and principals about how they can improve instruction; (3) Recruiting, developing, rewarding, and retaining effective teachers and principals, especially where they are needed most; and (4) Turning around our lowest-achieving schools" (U.S. Department of Education, 2009).

Though state agendas may vary somewhat in their implementation approach, common derivatives of these federal reform areas have manifested themselves into (a) new teacher and administrator evaluation programs, (b) STEM-based curriculum initiatives, (c) expanded data systems to support instruction, and (d) school reform initiatives. The reader will learn in the ensuing chapters that the above-mentioned priorities collectively retain common elements paramount for all digital age learners—emphasis on higher levels of student cognition, focus on engaging students, attention to solving real-world problems, and targeted technology use in the classroom.

Marzano (2012) calls this educational phenomenon the "converging evidence of research findings impacting student achievement." There is no longer one program (as if there ever was) that can be called the "total solution." Every new teacher evaluation system, STEM-based instructional unit, school reform model, or technology integration strategy has advantages and disadvantages depending on the manner and fidelity of its implementation cycle, yet they all have their genesis either directly or indirectly in empirical research that supports student achievement and improved classroom pedagogy.

The Digital Age Best Practices ranging from networked collaboration to formative assessment practices can be traced to any of these local, state, or federal initiatives impacting student achievement in the classroom. As Figure D illustrates, Digital Age Best Practices are aligned to the most popular teacher evaluation systems, most notably the *INTASC Core Teaching Standards*; STEM-based initiatives, which had their early roots in STS (Science Technology Society) research; 21st Century Skills; technology integration frameworks, including LoTi (Levels of Teaching Innovation), TPACK (Technological Pedagogical Content Knowledge), and SAMR (substitution, augmentation, modification, redefinition); school reform initiatives; and classroom walkthrough protocols, including the H.E.A.T. walkthrough system.

Chapter 8 will delve into a specific breakdown of each of these national and state initiatives driving school change efforts and their alignment to Digital Age Best Practices. Again, the notion of converging evidence will be used both to console and encourage those who perceive a machine-gun approach overtaking the educational landscape. Chapter 9 will tie change efforts directly to a case study of one urban school system, Atlantic City Public Schools, and their grassroots effort to implement Digital Age Best Practices in light of social, financial, and environmental issues that continue to challenge many urban school systems.

Figure D   DABP Bubble Map

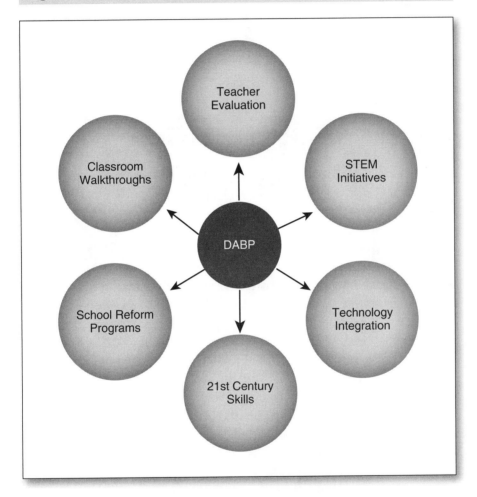

8

A National Perspective

School reform cynics have often referenced the lack of meaningful change in classroom instructional practices despite substantial federal (e.g., NCLB, IDEA, ESEA) support and increases in state funding over the years. The primary source of federal K–12 support first began in 1965 with the enactment of the *Elementary and Secondary Education Act (ESEA)*. Yet, what meaningful impact has this funding made on teaching and learning over the years?

The erratic nature of educational reform, especially at the secondary level, has too frequently been criticized in scholarly books, educational journals, and blog posts, and it has served as the unfortunate punch line for popular jokes (e.g., *If you were in a time capsule and went back in time 100 years, where would you feel most at home—a high school classroom!*). This is not to say that the criticism has been unwarranted. Pedagogical inertia, quick fix solutions to high stake testing woes, feeble attempts at implementing quality technology integration, and vacillating district-level priorities have reinforced the status quo and perpetuated a conventional pedagogy in most K–12 classrooms nationwide.

As Wallace and Pocklington (2002) remind us, complex educational change is nonlinear. Yet, how often has there ever been that "perfect wave" in which stakeholder expectations, available funding sources, targeted professional development, and time dedicated to the change effort are in sync with one another? Most implementations, whether a new math textbook adoption or a new teacher evaluation system, attempt to find a minimum level of acceptable fidelity to the actual guiding innovation.

A plethora of recent educational initiatives illustrate this point. The proliferation of digital resources in our nation's classroom during the past twenty-five years was accomplished primarily by assembling and submitting a required technology plan to a state agency in return for receiving dollars for technology. The result was the installation of laptop stations and carts, interactive whiteboards, and mobile devices (e.g., BYOD—bring your own device) that complemented and perpetuated the existing instructional curriculum. One could argue that the placement of technology in U.S. K–12 schools has represented one of the biggest smoke screens to hit public education in the last fifty years. Why? Because isolated technology use in the classroom often hides what is not happening—collaborative and inquiry-based learning, higher-order thinking, and real-world problem solving—the cornerstones of 21st Century Skills.

The recent adoption of new teacher evaluation systems resulting from *Race to the Top* funding is another in a long line of educational innovations (e.g., minimum competency testing, outcome-based education, No Child Left Behind [NCLB]) that have experienced initial broad appeal because of their timeliness and/or pedagogical merit, but their actual implementation has often stranded or discontinued other viable programs in the district in favor of the newest arrival. In the case of new teacher evaluation systems, some districts have either discontinued or limited their focus on competing professional development priorities (e.g., differentiated instruction, collaborative learning, real-world problem solving, classroom walkthroughs) so that the majority of resources could concentrate on the current brand.

Vacillating among competing initiatives or "switching channels" sends mixed signals to critical stakeholders (e.g., building administrators, teachers, parents), which creates a growing pessimism about the importance of any district initiative, promotes passive resistance among the rank and file, and ultimately perpetuates the conventional operational curriculum. This is not to say that abandoning one program for another is necessarily a bad decision as long as quantitative (e.g., test scores results, changes in instructional practices, funding) and/or qualitative results (e.g., survey feedback, personal interviews) suggest a different course of action.

Attempting to locate quick-fix solutions for deep-seated problems further obstructs the change process. The passage of the landmark

NCLB in 2001 is a classic case study in over-reacting to a new mandate or law. Though the NCLB bill required public schools to report publicly student academic progress in mathematics and reading, the implementation approach used by many school systems ignored what current research tells us about how students learn best. The predominant use of didactic instruction coupled with over-testing students (sometimes weekly) on low-level skills in order to show growth on isolated content embedded in the standards completely ignores research-best practices tied to student achievement.

As the reader will learn in Chapter 12, the issue is not so much with new federal legislation or new local mandates, but in the decision-making process used by key stakeholders responsible for their implementation. Part of the problem is the lack of clarity or perhaps understanding as to how seemingly conflicting initiatives have their foundational support in a common set of best practices.

So where is the converging evidence with many of these current educational initiatives that on the surface appear disconnected yet underneath support the critical elements of Digital Age Best Practices? What follows is a summary of many popular curriculum and instructional initiatives that directly or indirectly align with Digital Age Best Practices.

New Teacher Evaluation Systems

Implementation of new teacher evaluation systems across the country vary in their approach, yet most have as their foundation the *INTASC Core Teaching Standards* developed by the Council of Chief State School Officers (2011). These standards outline what teachers across all content and grade levels should know and be able to do to be effective in today's learning environments. The INTASC Standards provide specific guidelines for school systems to design teacher evaluation criteria that are research based, promote 21st Century Skills and Themes, and address the needs of all digital age learners.

When asked how the INTASC Standards aligned to Digital Age Best Practices, the reoccurring theme of converging evidence surfaces. A careful inspection of these standards reveals a high degree of alignment in critical areas of classroom instruction including preparation, differentiation, learning environments, and instructional strategies.

The Digital Age Best Practice *Accelerating individual growth through vertical/horizontal differentiation* compares favorably with INTASC Standard 1 (Learner Development), Standard 2 (Learning

Differences), Standard 7 (Planning for Instruction), and Standard 10 (Leadership and Collaboration). These standards articulate the importance of understanding individual differences, designing learning experiences that are developmentally appropriate and challenging, supporting an individual student's achievement of rigorous standards, and above all, planning professional development opportunities that address the needs of individual learners.

The Digital Age Best Practice *Bolstering purposeful inquiry through student questions* aligns closely with INTASC Standard 1 (Learning Development), Standard 4 (Content Knowledge), and Standard 5 (Application of Content) and their collective emphasis on challenging learning experiences that make use of student inquiry, critical thinking, and collaborative problem solving. Finally, the Digital Age Best Practice *Personalizing and globalizing content by making authentic connection* is consistent with INTASC Standard 4 (Content Knowledge), Standard 5 (Application of Content), and Standard 8 (Instructional Strategies). Both schema emphasize making student learning real, relevant, and applicable at both the local and global levels.

The danger with rolling out an initiative such as a new teacher evaluation system is the potential push back from key stakeholders (e.g., teachers) when competing and, in many instances, complementary initiatives and professional development opportunities are compromised or eliminated so that everyone can focus on the newest "flavor of the month." As Figure 8.0 illustrates, many of the domains embedded in the INTASC Standards directly align with Digital Age Best Practices; yet complementary district professional development programs that may be catching steam among staff members, including differentiated instruction, questioning strategies, and technology integration, may be lost or eliminated because of a district or campus decision maker's inability to connect the dots and recognize the common threads that bind all of these initiatives together.

Technology Integration Practices

Technology integration practices frequently vary from classroom to classroom and school to school depending on several variables (e.g., access to hardware, available professional development, administrator expectations). Several technology integration frameworks currently offer educational practitioners a means of assessing effective technology use practices using a graduated scale. Some of the more popular frameworks include LoTi, TIM (Technology Integration

Matrix), TPACK, and SAMR (Substitution, Augmentation, Modification, and Redefinition).

The LoTi framework was first conceptualized by Moersch (1994) as a research tool to assess authentic classroom technology use. Several iterations later, the original framework was modified to measure a classroom teacher's implementation of the tenets of digital age literacy as manifested in the National Educational Technology Standards for Teachers (NETS-T). Figure 8.0 outlines the LoTi framework and its alignment to Digital Age Best Practices.

Though any of the above frameworks provides an acceptable methodology for quantifying technology use in the classroom, the LoTi framework is highlighted in particular because (a) the framework represents a statistically valid indicator of effective technology integration practices, (b) the framework is researched-based, and (c) the framework has experienced broad appeal within the research community worldwide as a way of quantifying technology integration practices in the classroom. As with the INTASC Standards, the LoTi framework is tightly coupled to the tenets of Digital Age Best Practices starting at LoTi Level 3.

Figure 8.0   LoTi Levels

LoTi Level 0: Nonuse

At a level 0 (nonuse), the instructional setting—including the use of digital and/or environmental resources—does not support or promote purposeful learning aligned to academic standards/expectations.

LoTi Level 1: Awareness

At a level 1 (Awareness), the instructional focus is exclusively direct instruction. Student learning focuses on lower levels of cognitive processing (e.g., Bloom levels—remembering, understanding, applying; Webb's levels—recall and reproduction, working with skills and concepts). Digital and/or environmental resources are either (a) nonexistent or (b) used by the classroom teacher to enhance teacher lectures or presentations (e.g., multimedia presentations).

LoTi Level 2: Exploration

At a level 2 (Exploration), the instructional focus emphasizes content understanding and supports mastery learning and direct instruction. Student learning focuses on lower levels of cognitive processing (e.g., Bloom levels—remembering, understanding, applying; Webb's levels—recall and reproduction, working with skills and concepts). Digital and/or environmental resources are used by students for extension activities, enrichment exercises, or information gathering assignments that reinforce lower cognitive skill development relating to the content under investigation.

LoTi Level 3: Infusion

At a level 3 (Infusion), the instructional focus emphasizes student higher-order thinking (e.g., Bloom levels—analyzing, evaluating, creating; Webb's levels—short-term strategic thinking) and teacher-directed problems. Though specific learning activities may lack authenticity, the instructional emphasis is, nonetheless, placed on higher levels of cognitive processing and in-depth treatment of the content using a variety of thinking skill strategies (e.g., problem solving, decision making). The concept attainment, inductive thinking, and scientific inquiry models of teaching are the norm and guide the types of products generated by students.

Digital and/or environmental resources are used by students and/or the teacher to execute teacher-directed tasks that emphasize higher levels of student cognitive processing relating to the content under investigation.

DABP Alignment

- **Bolsters purposeful inquiry through student questions**
- **Promotes shared expertise with networked collaboration**
- **Anchors student learning with digital age tools and resources**

LoTi Level 4a: Integration (Mechanical)

At a level 4a (Integration: Mechanical) students are engaged in exploring real-world issues and solving authentic problems using the available digital and/or environmental resources; however, the teacher may experience classroom management (e.g., disciplinary problems) or school climate issues (lack of support from colleagues) that restrict full-scale integration. Heavy reliance is placed on prepackaged materials and/or outside resources (e.g., assistance from other colleagues) that aid the teacher in sustaining engaged student-directed learning. Emphasis is placed on the constructivist, problem-based models of teaching that require higher levels of student cognitive processing (e.g., Bloom levels—analyzing, evaluating, creating; Webb's levels—short-term strategic thinking, extended strategic thinking) and in-depth examination of the content.

Student use of digital and/or environmental resources is inherent and motivated by the drive to answer student-generated questions that

(Continued)

Figure 8.0 (Continued)

dictate the content, process, and/or products embedded in the learning experience.

DABP Alignment

- **Bolsters purposeful inquiry through student questions**
- **Personalizes and globalizes content by making authentic connections**
- **Anchors student learning with digital age tools and resources**
- **Implements student-centered learning environments**

LoTi Level 4b: Integration (Routine)

At a level 4b (Integration: Routine) students are fully engaged in exploring real-world issues and solving authentic problems using the available digital and/or environmental resources. The teacher is within his or her comfort level with promoting an inquiry-based model of teaching that involves students applying their learning to the real world (e.g., Webb's levels—extended strategic thinking). Emphasis is placed on learner-centered strategies and the constructivist, problem-based models of teaching that promote personal goal setting and self-monitoring, student action, and issues resolution.

Students use of digital and/or environmental resources is inherent and motivated by the drive to answer student-generated questions that dictate the content, process, and products embedded in the learning experience.

DABP Alignment

- **Bolsters purposeful inquiry through student questions**
- **Personalizes and globalizes content by making authentic connections**
- **Anchors student learning with digital age tools and resources**
- **Implements student-centered learning environments**

LoTi Level 5: Expansion

At a level 5 (Expansion), student collaborations extending beyond the classroom are employed for authentic problem solving and issues resolution. Emphasis is placed on learner-centered strategies that promote personal goal setting and self-monitoring, student action, and collaborations with other groups (e.g., another school, different cultures, business establishments, governmental agencies).

Student use of digital and/or environmental resources is inherent and motivated by the drive to answer student-generated questions that dictate the content, process, and products embedded in the learning experience. The complexity and sophistication of the digital and environmental resources and collaboration tools used are commensurate with (a) the inventiveness and spontaneity of the teacher's experiential-based approach to teaching and learning and (b) the students' level of complex thinking (e.g., problem solving, decision making, experimental inquiry) and in-depth understanding of the content experienced in the classroom.

DABP Alignment

- **Bolsters purposeful inquiry through student questions**
- **Promotes shared expertise with networked collaboration**
- **Personalizes and globalizes content by making authentic connections**
- **Accelerates individual growth through vertical/horizontal differentiation**
- **Anchors student learning with digital age tools and resources**
- **Implements student-centered learning environments**

LoTi Level 6: Refinement

At a level 6 (Refinement), student collaborations extending beyond the classroom that promote authentic student problem solving and issues resolution are the norm. The instructional curriculum is entirely learner based, involving the content, process, and product of instruction. The content emerges based on the needs of the learner according to his or her interests and/or aspirations and is supported by pervasive access to the most current digital resources.

The pervasive use of and access to advanced digital resources provides a seamless medium for information queries, creative problem solving, student reflection, and/or product development. Students have ready access to and a complete understanding of a vast array of collaboration tools and related resources to accomplish learning outcomes beyond conventional strategies.

DABP Alignment

- **Bolsters purposeful inquiry through student questions**
- **Promotes shared expertise with networked collaboration**
- **Personalizes and globalizes content by making authentic connections**
- **Accelerates individual growth through vertical/horizontal differentiation**
- **Anchors student learning with digital age tools and resources**
- **Implements student-centered learning environments**

Source: Reprinted with permission from *Learning & Leading with Technology*, vol. 37, no. 5 © 2010, ISTE® (International Society for Technology in Education), www.iste.org.

Standards-Based Instruction

Standards-based school reform became a predominant issue facing public schools as early as 1983 with the publication of *A Nation at Risk*; the recent release of the Common Core State Standards has refocused attention on this issue. The basis of school reform has been largely driven by the setting of academic standards for what students should know and be able to do at the end of an instructional episode or unit. The entire standards-based instruction movement is predicated on providing clear, measurable standards for all school students.

Ainsworth and Viegut (2006) offer a succinct conceptual model for designing any standards-based instruction and assessment process. Their approach is comprised of six stages that offer a cyclical loop for continuous feedback and refinement of instructional practices and student interventions (see Figure 8.1).

Steps C and F readily emphasize the importance of formative and summative assessments and the subsequent decision-making process used to drive follow-up interventions and pathways for acceleration. These steps clearly support the Digital Age Best Practice *Clarifying student understanding with formative assessments*.

Step D (i.e., instructional unit design) may vary among a school system's use of standards-based instruction based on any number of variables (e.g., subject matter concerns, district/campus leadership, evaluation tools); yet, the more popular instructional design models (e.g., Universal Design for Learning [UDL], 5E Model, Self-regulated Learning [SRL], Understanding by Design) collectively abide by a set of common components that support Digital Age Best Practices. Figure 8.2 provides a sample combination UDL/SRL lesson plan that seamlessly integrates each of the Digital Age Best Practices.

High-Stakes Testing

Efforts to increase student academic achievement as determined by high-stakes tests has occupied the majority of the public education's collective psyche since the passage of NCLB in 2001. Many school systems leverage their last remaining grant dollars and/or federal funding allocations to squeeze a few more percentage points out of students relating to raising test scores, often to the detriment of other initiatives. Yet, it is the implementation of these other competing initiatives at a high level of fidelity that can make the difference in

Figure 8.1   Stages of Standards-Based Instruction

A. Power standards

B. Unwrapping the standards, big ideas, and essential questions

C. Formative and summative assessments

DABP Alignment

- **Clarifies student understanding with formative assessments**

D. Instructional unit design, including classroom performance assessments (e.g., UDL Model)

DABP Alignment

- **Bolsters purposeful inquiry through student questions**
- **Promotes shared expertise with networked collaboration**
- **Personalizes and globalizes content by making authentic connections**
- **Accelerates individual growth through vertical/horizontal differentiation**
- **Anchors student learning with digital age tools and resources**
- **Clarifies student understanding with formative assessments**
- **Implements student-centered learning environments**

E. Collaborative scoring of student work, including implications for grading

F. Data-driving instructional decision making, including implications for interventions and acceleration

DABP Alignment

- **Clarifies student understanding with formative assessments**
- **Accelerates individual growth through vertical/horizontal differentiation**

students' maximizing what they know and are able to do on standardized tests.

In Section I, a similar argument was made on behalf of each of the Digital Age Best Practices both as a theoretical construct and as a practical application in terms of promoting increased student achievement while providing the necessary empirical support for existing district or campus initiatives.

Figure 8.2 Lesson Plan: Mathematics: Which Sport Is the Hardest to Play?

Subject and Unit Title	Mathematics: Which Sport Is the Hardest to Play?
Grade Level	Grade 7
Unit Description	Students investigate the geometric concepts of area and circumference of a circle and use them to solve a real-world problem.
Lesson Description	In this lesson, students apply their understanding of area and circumference to determine in which sport it is the most difficult to score a point by comparing the ratio of the circumference and area of an athletic ball (e.g., basketball, golf ball, soccer ball, water polo ball) to the circumference/perimeter and area of the receiving goal/net (e.g., basketball hoop, cup, net).
Provincial Prescribed Learning Outcomes	CCSS: 7.G.4. Know the formulas for the area and circumference of a circle and use them to solve problems; give an informal derivation of the relationship between the circumference and area of a circle.

1. Lesson Goals	To broaden student's ability to contextualize fundamental math concepts (ratio, fractions, pi) across all math strands.			
SRL Component	☑ Complex Task	☑ Choices	☑ Control Over Challenge	☑ Cooperative Learning	☑ Reflective Activity

DABP Alignment

- **Bolsters purposeful inquiry through student questions**
- **Promotes shared expertise with networked collaboration**
- **Accelerates individual growth through vertical/horizontal differentiation**
- **Implements student-centered learning environment**

Methods

2. Prelesson Activity	Share with students that ESPN has recently conducted a poll to determine peoples' opinion about which sport is most difficult to perform.
	Have groups of four students rotate through a series of game stations to become familiar with making a goal, point, or putt using five different online simulators. These simulators include water polo, basketball, volleyball, golf, and soccer.
	Pose the question, "Is it easier to make a 15-foot shot with a basketball or a 15-foot putt with a golf club?"
	Have students rank order five different sports from easiest to hardest to score a point.
Introduce and Model New Knowledge	Tell students that they will be testing ESPN's rankings mathematically by (a) comparing the circumference or perimeter of the goal, basketball rim, golf cup, and so forth, with the circumference of the ball used in each sport and (b) using a decision-making matrix to determine their own ranking of the five sports from easiest to hardest based on their own categories; for example, ratio, endurance, challenge, danger.
	Have students measure the circumference of a soccer ball, water polo ball, basketball, golf ball, and hockey puck. On the board, write the circumference/perimeter of the goal, basketball rim, and so forth that aligns to each of the five selected sports.
	Have students work in pairs to determine the ratio of the circumference of the basketball rim to the circumference of the basketball.

Figure 8.2 (Continued)

Introduce and Model New Knowledge (continued)	After students have correctly calculated the ratio of the basketball rim to the basketball, provide them with a series of questions to help them contextualize their understanding of circumference of a circle through follow-up questions such as the following:
	• If the basketball was a Nerf basketball with a diameter of 5 inches, what would be the circumference ratio of the basketball rim to the Nerf basketball?
	• If the basketball rim had a 25% larger diameter, what would be the circumference ratio of the basketball rim to the original basketball?
	• Based on the circumference of the original basketball, what is its area?
	• Based on the circumference of the original basketball rim, what is its area?
Guided Practice	Assign students to a small breakout group or center if they are experiencing difficulty with calculating the ratio of the circumference of the rim, cup, net, or goal to the circumference of the ball or puck.
	Use any of the websites below to review ratios and circumference/area with students:
	• Ratios
	http://www.math.com/school/subject1/practice/S1U2L1/S1U2L1Pract.html
	http://math.rice.edu/~lanius/proportions/
	http://www.galaxygoo.org/math/allAboutRatios.html
	• Circumference of a circle
	http://www.mathopenref.com/circumference.html
	http://illuminations.nctm.org/ActivityDetail.aspx?id=116
	• Area of a circle
	http://www.mathgoodies.com/lessons/vol2/circle_area.html

Independent Practice	Have students work in pairs to determine the ratio of the circumference/perimeter of the goal to the circumference of the ball for each of the four remaining sports.

After students have correctly calculated the ratio of the goal to the ball expressed as a fraction for each of the four remaining sports, provide them with a series of questions to help them contextualize their understanding of circumference of a circle through follow-up questions:

- If the soccer goal had a diameter 3/4 the size of its current diameter, what would be the ratio of the perimeter of the soccer goal to the soccer ball (circumference)?
- If the ice hockey goal had a 25% larger diameter, what would be the ratio of the perimeter of the hockey goal to the hockey puck (circumference)?

Have students complete a decision-making matrix for the five sports. This matrix or grid will help students determine a mathematical ranking of the sports based on specific criteria. First, the students will need to brainstorm different criteria or categories that should be used to rank order sports from easiest to hardest. Some possible categories (besides the ratio of the circumference/perimeter of the goal to the circumference of the ball) include risk level, stress, endurance, and/or strength.

Note: *One of the categories, ratio, needs to be used because it serves as the focal point for the entire lesson. Let the students choose the remaining categories based on their experiences.* |

(Continued)

Figure 8.2 (Continued)

Independent Practice (continued)	Have students rank order the sports from (1) Easiest to (5) Hardest for each of the categories. For example, a sport with a ratio of 1:2 representing the ratio of the circumference/perimeter of the goal to the circumference of the ball would be ranked "harder" than a sport with a ratio of 1:50. In other words, it may be more difficult to sink a golf ball into a golf cup with a 1:2 ratio of golf cup to golf ball than to kick a soccer ball (with no defenders or goalie) into a soccer net with a 1:50 ratio of the soccer goal to the soccer ball.
	Have students add the totals for each sport and then rank order them based on the point totals.
Wrap Up	Have students compose a class blog post to an ESPN blog that allows individuals to share their comments. Require students to explain mathematically how they arrived at their conclusions related to their mathematical rankings.

DABP Alignment

- **Bolsters purposeful inquiry through student questions**
- **Promotes shared expertise with networked collaboration**
- **Personalizes and globalizes content by making authentic connections**
- **Clarifies student understanding with formative assessments**

Assessment

Formative/Ongoing Assessment	During the activity that prompts students to determine the ratio of various athletic balls to their correspondence goal/net, be sure to note which students have trouble determining the ratio for each sport.
Summative/End of Lesson Assessment	Have students complete the exit card for the lesson.

DABP Alignment

- **Clarifies student understanding with formative assessments**

Materials

- ESPN

  http://www.espn.com

- Netblazer

  http://www.learn4good.com/games/sports/basketball_netblazer.htm

- Mini Putt

  http://www.cuteflashgames.com/game/mini_putt.html

- Free KickMania

  http://fifasoccer.ru/en/flash/play/?what=freekickmania

- Online volleyball

  http://www.bubbletoonia.com/game/volleyball.html

- Sports game: water polo

  http://www.playflashgamez.com/game/717/water-polo

- PowerPoint: Sports and Circumference

- Hockey puck

DABP Alignment

- **Anchors student learning with digital age tools and resources**

Webb's Depth of Knowledge (DOK) Framework

This framework (Mississippi Department of Education, 2009) provides a common vocabulary on a graduated scale when ascertaining how students engage with the content. DOK offers a common language to understand "rigor" or cognitive demand in assessments, curricular units, and lesson plans. The four DOK levels that grow in cognitive complexity and provide educators a lens on creating more cognitively engaging and challenging tasks include

Level 1: Recall and Reproduction

Level 2: Working With Skills and Concepts

Level 3: Short-Term Strategic Thinking

Level 4: Extended Strategic Thinking

DABP Alignment

- **Bolsters purposeful inquiry through student questions**
- **Promotes shared expertise with networked collaboration**

Daggett's Rigor and Relevance Framework

Daggett's Rigor and Relevance Framework (International Center for Research in Education): The Rigor/Relevance Framework examines curriculum, instruction, and assessment practices using two separate yet converging constructs: "rigor" and "relevance." The rigor of knowledge taxonomy is a continuum based on the revised levels of Bloom's taxonomy; the relevance or application model includes graduated levels of applied learning. The Rigor/Relevance Framework is comprised of four quadrants that characterize the learning or student performance at that level.

DABP Alignment

- **Bolsters purposeful inquiry through student questions**
- **Promotes shared expertise with networked collaboration**
- **Personalizes and globalizes content by making authentic connections**
- **Implements student-centered learning environments**

Gardner Multiple Intelligences

The Multiple Intelligences Model (Gardner, 2011) conceptualized by Gardner suggests that there exists eight unique "intelligences" that learners possess that impacts how they receive and process information;

- Linguistic intelligence: a sensitivity to the meaning and order of words
- Logical-mathematical intelligence: ability in mathematics and other complex logical systems
- Musical intelligence: the ability to understand and create music
- Spatial intelligence: the ability to "think in pictures," to perceive the visual world accurately, and re-create (or alter) it in the mind or on paper
- Bodily-kinesthetic intelligence: the ability to use one's body in a skilled way, for self-expression or toward a goal
- Interpersonal intelligence: an ability to perceive and understand other individuals—their moods, desires, and motivations
- Intrapersonal intelligence: an understanding of one's own emotions
- Naturalist intelligence: ability to recognize and classify plants, minerals, and animals, including rocks and grass and all variety of flora and fauna

DABP Alignment

- **Accelerates individual growth through vertical/horizontal differentiation**

21st Century Skills

The 21st Century Skills framework (Partnership for the 21st Century) articulates a set of skills needed by learners to function successfully in a global work environment. These skill sets include

1. Learning and innovation skills
   - Creativity and innovation
   - Critical thinking and problem solving
   - Communication and collaboration

2. Information, media, and technology skills
   - Information literacy
   - Media literacy
   - ICT literacy

3. Life and career skills

DABP Alignment

- Bolsters purposeful inquiry through student questions
- Promotes shared expertise with networked collaboration
- Personalizes and globalizes content by making authentic connections
- Anchors student learning with digital age tools and resources
- Implements student-centered learning environments

SUMMARY

Chapter 8 concentrated on connecting the dots between current national initiatives driving school change efforts and Digital Age Best Practices. Gaining a deeper understanding of the empirical support of these initiatives and other worthy change efforts not mentioned in this book may help to prevent knee-jerk reactions to the latest innovation on the educational horizon. Chapter 9 will discuss how one urban school system, the Atlantic City Public Schools, channeled their collective energies into implementing programs, protocols, and procedures that aligned to Digital Age Best Practices and helped to transform their school system into a high-performing district.

9

The Atlantic City Experience

The Atlantic City Board of Education's (ACBOE) story is best illustrated by the theme of converging forces coming together simultaneously to impact positively all facets of the institutional curriculum. The dramatic increases in student academic achievement did not happen overnight but did show sufficient progress that provided needed momentum and empirical support to maintain the current course of action. Programs were not abandoned for the sake of personal preference or because they did not generate instant results; rather, each program was evaluated annually based on its merits and alignment to the bigger picture—a picture shared by all key stakeholders.

The bigger picture in this case extended beyond achieving adequate yearly progress (AYP) or safe harbor (represents a 10% reduction in the number of students not passing the statewide assessments) in mathematics and literacy for a particular grade level or student subpopulation, but it included both quantitative and qualitative indicators, such as student and teacher attendance rates, positive school climate, community satisfaction, and increased high school graduation rates. District leaders worked closely with parent and student groups, the teacher's union, and vendors to ensure a high level of fidelity and success among the various initiatives (e.g., literacy collaborative, technology purchases, math benchmarking) impacting the teaching and learning process.

This chapter highlights these key initiatives employed by the ACBOE and their alignment to Digital Age Best Practices.

Benchmarking Process

One of the pivotal changes made in the ACBOE's math curriculum was the development of standards-aligned benchmarks that provided specific guidelines for third- through eighth-grade teachers relating to the math content and specifically to the New Jersey Assessment of Skills and Knowledge (NJ ASK) test specifications and the Common Core State Standards (CCSS). The math benchmarks were developed by the district's math committee, comprised of lead teachers, district math coaches, and the supervisor of mathematics and assessment.

Special attention was given to ensuring the presence of four specific criteria paramount to a successful benchmarking process: (1) possesses the look and feel of the actual statewide assessment, (2) measures what has already been taught, (3) ensures an efficient turn-around time for data analysis and summary, and (4) provides follow-up interventions for students at a LoTi 3+. Ensuring that all follow-up interventions targeted a LoTi 3+ was consistent with the district's efforts to elevate student engagement across the curriculum.

The use of the benchmarking process targeted the Digital Age Best Practice *Clarify student understanding with formative assessments.* As mentioned in Chapter 8, executing student-learning experiences at a LoTi 3 aligns with three Digital Age Best Practices: *Bolstering purposeful inquiry through student questions, Promoting shared expertise with networked collaboration,* and *Anchoring student learning with digital-age tools and resources.*

One of the popular myths associated with the entire math benchmarking process is that students need to understand underlying math fundamentals, such as the four basic operations (i.e., adding, subtracting, multiplying, dividing), number representation, and conversions (e.g., converting fractions to decimals), before moving to more advanced math concepts. The Atlantic City benchmarking process took a different path relating to these math fundamentals. The focus was on students contextualizing rather than simply understanding the math fundamentals within the benchmarking process so that students could visualize how the same math concepts are interwoven across different math strands.

Figure 9.0 provides a simple illustration of contextualizing the math concept, fractions, across each of the Math Common Core State Standards.

Contextualizing these math fundamentals across the CCSS domains through a variety of outlets (benchmark tests, skill builders or problems-of-the-day, LoTi 3 math investigations) (a) provided an expansive informal assessment process to ensure that students were able to apply or transfer these foundational skills and concepts to a new context; (b) prevented staff members from dwelling on a

Figure 9.0   Math Common Core State Standards—Grade 6

Ratios and Proportional Relationships	The Number System
CCSS.Math.Content.6.RP.A.2 Understand the concept of a unit rate $\frac{a}{b}$ associated with a ratio $a{:}b$ with $b \neq 0$, and use rate language in the context of a ratio relationship. *For example,* George has 5 times as many marbles as Gracie. What is the ratio of the number of marbles Gracie has to George's marbles?	CCSS.Math.Content.6.NS.A.1 Interpret and compute quotients of fractions, and solve word problems involving division of fractions by fractions, e.g., by using visual fraction models and equations to represent the problem. *For example,* How many $\frac{3}{4}$-cup servings are in $\frac{2}{3}$ of a cup of yogurt?
Expressions and Equations	**Statistics and Probability**
CCSS.Math.Content.6.EE.B.7 Solve real-world and mathematical problems by writing and solving equations of the form $x + p = q$ and $px = q$ for cases in which p, q and x are all nonnegative rational numbers. *For example,* Solve for x ($px = q$).	CCSS.Math.Content.6.SP.A.3 Recognize that a measure of center for a numerical data set summarizes all of its values with a single number, while a measure of variation describes how its values vary with a single number. *For example,* What is the mean of the following measurements: $\frac{3}{4}''$, $1\frac{1}{2}''$, $2''$, and $3\frac{1}{4}''$?

Source: Common Core State Standards (2010)

particular math concept, such as adding or subtracting fractions, in isolation; and (c) ensured that all staff members were teaching within the same math cluster throughout the school year.

H.E.A.R.T. Walkthroughs

The district created a unique classroom walkthrough protocol using the acronym H.E.A.R.T. to monitor and quantify critical attributes of teaching and learning in the classroom. H.E.A.R.T. is a slightly morphed version of Moersch's original H.E.A.T. (Higher-Order Thinking, Engaged Learning, Authentic Connections, Technology Use) Framework (Moersch, 2010) with the addition of the *R* representing rubrics. The Classroom Walkthrough with H.E.A.T. protocol was originally created to capture and document the amount of student H.E.A.T. in the classroom. Figure 9.1 provides an alignment of the original H.E.A.T. Framework to each of the Digital Age Best Practices.

Research supports the concept that classroom walkthroughs assume a positive role in reflective practice and continuous improvement efforts (Downey & Frase, 2001; Downey, Steffy, English, Frase, &

Figure 9.1   H.E.A.T. Framework and Digital Age Best Practices Graphic Organizer

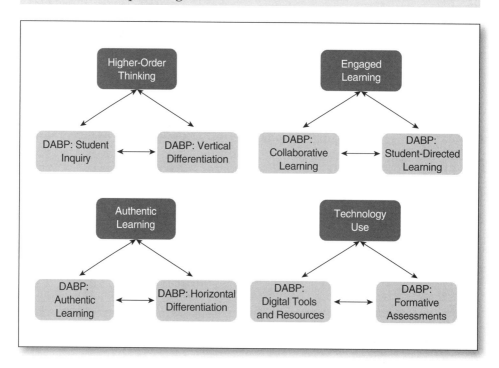

Posten, 2004; Elmore, 2000). According to Hall and Hord (2000), class-room walkthroughs that include focused one-on-one feedback are the most powerful staff development approach available to impact and change behavior. However, David (2008) cautions us that "walk-throughs can play a constructive role only when districts make their purpose clear and carry them out in a climate of trust" (p. 82).

The Classroom Walkthrough with H.E.A.R.T. process used in the ACBOE represents a hybrid of several current walkthrough approaches articulated in Kachur, Stout, and Edwards' *Classroom Walkthroughs to Improve Teaching and Learning* (2010) and includes five steps: pre-walkthrough, H.E.A.R.T. Walkthrough, post-walkthrough, group data analysis, and group action plan.

The Classroom Walkthrough with H.E.A.R.T. form used in the district integrated the critical H.E.A.R.T. look-fors as well as the state of New Jersey compliance guidelines referred to as CAPA (Collabora-tive Assessment for Planning and Achievement). These guidelines outlined specific areas of the instructional process that required ongo-ing monitoring as mandated by the New Jersey Department of Edu-cation. A summary of the five-step classroom walkthroughs with H.E.A.R.T. protocol follows.

Step 1: Pre-Walkthrough

According to the Center for Comprehensive School Reform and Improvement (2007), a classroom walkthrough is defined as a brief, structured, non-evaluative classroom observation by a principal that is followed by a conversation between the principal and the teacher about what was observed. Though walkthroughs represent unan-nounced classroom visitations, it is essential that campus leaders plan with a focus or purpose in mind. According to Downey et al. (2004), this focus should include a consideration of curriculum (e.g., math benchmarks, new reading program, differentiated instruction) as well as instructional initiatives (e.g., adequate wait time, questioning strat-egies).

In the ACBOE, this focus included an inspection of the H.E.A.R.T. Look-fors embedded in the H.E.A.R.T. Walkthrough form, a review of prior H.E.A.R.T. Walkthrough reports, and a consideration of current curriculum initiatives on campus. Since H.E.A.R.T. represents student output and is synonymous with 21st Century Skills, it was pivotal that district and building leaders possessed a thorough understand-ing of the H.E.A.R.T. look-fors to ensure maximum validity and reli-ability with their classroom observations.

Reviewing prior H.E.A.R.T. Walkthrough reports and considering current curriculum initiatives ensured that building leaders encapsulated a purposeful intent for their classroom visits. For example, if prior walkthrough reports revealed a need to implement more informal assessment strategies by a particular teacher, then the follow-up walkthrough in this teacher's classroom by the building leader would focus on specific informal assessment techniques used in the classroom, such as choral responses, hand signaling, Think-Pair-Share, or exit cards.

The same is true with existing curriculum initiatives at the campus level. One of the advantages of the walkthrough process in the ACBOE was to ensure that curriculum programs, such as the math benchmark process, were implemented with a high degree of fidelity. Addressing both the content (e.g., math benchmarks, standards-based instruction) and instructional priorities (e.g., questioning strategies, differentiated instruction, higher order thinking) during a Classroom Walkthrough with H.E.A.R.T. created an implied level of expectation on behalf of the administrator as well as the teacher.

Step 2: H.E.A.R.T. Walkthrough

How long should a walkthrough last? Three minutes? Five minutes? Fifteen minutes? Classroom walkthrough strategists offer their own perspective on the acceptable time period of a walkthrough. The Downey classroom walkthrough model suggests two to three minutes; other protocols range from one to twenty-five minutes depending on the scope and frequency of the walkthrough process (Kachur et al., 2010).

In the Classroom Walkthrough with H.E.A.R.T. protocol, the recommended time period was approximately five minutes depending on the availability of classroom artifacts (e.g., student work samples, teacher/student exchanges, availability of lesson plans). The intent was to collect as much data as necessary during the brief classroom snapshot to ascertain the amount of student H.E.A.R.T. generated from the entire instructional episode. In this manner, the walkthrough process was not dependent on arriving in the classroom at the "right" time.

How often have we heard from disgruntled teachers who became frustrated because their administrator came in at the wrong time, perhaps missing an important dialogue or interaction between the teacher and students or among the students pertaining to the content? By focusing attention on corroborating the Gestalt of the entire instructional episode (e.g., class period) during a five minute data-gathering period involving observation, informal dialogue with the teacher and/or students (when convenient and appropriate), and a review of available classroom documents (e.g., posted rubrics, lesson plans, student work samples), a complete picture can be generated that, in turn, can provide a foundation for reflective practice and continuous improvement.

Step 3: Post-Walkthrough

The Classroom Walkthrough with H.E.A.R.T. post-walkthrough was the most critical and beneficial step for professional improvement in the ACBOE. Based on data collected from over five hundred K–12 classroom teachers in the district receiving a walkthrough from their administrators during the 2011 through 2012 school year, 89% reported that the administrative feedback was a useful part of the continuous improvement walkthrough process (e.g., positive, productive, promotes reflective practice) (LoTi Connection, 2012).

In the Classroom Walkthrough with H.E.A.R.T. protocol, the post-walkthrough process involved (a) creating a walkthrough summary highlighting the scope of the lesson and generating recommendations/commendations and (b) providing face-to-face feedback to the participating teacher(s). Using either a mobile device or a clipboard with a H.E.A.R.T. Walkthrough form attached, the administrator could automatically generate a H.E.A.R.T. Walkthrough summary report for the teacher based on the amount of student H.E.A.R.T. witnessed or verified during the classroom walkthrough experience.

This H.E.A.R.T. Walkthrough report provided the basis for an informal follow-up post-walkthrough conference between administrator and teacher that should occur immediately (if possible) but no more than five working days from the date of the walkthrough. This post-walkthrough conference was pivotal to the entire process. In the district, the type of dialogue ranged from a simple reflective question (e.g., How well do you think your students are grasping the content?) to a brief discussion surrounding a specific recommendation or commendation.

Step 4: Group Data Analysis

What sets apart the Classroom Walkthrough with H.E.A.R.T. protocol from other walkthrough methodologies was its focus on data analysis to promote system-wide, continuous improvement.

Aggregating the collected H.E.A.R.T. Walkthrough data over time enabled campus instructional leader(s) to identify trends in 21st Century Skill implementation (i.e., Higher order thinking, Engaged learning, Authentic connections, Technology use) that could potentially lead to adjustments in current professional development efforts and peer mentoring practices.

Figures 9.2 and 9.3 display pie charts aggregating data from two of the H.E.A.R.T. components, Engaged Learning and Technology Use, respectively, during the 2011 through 2012 school year.

The data in Figure 9.2 shows that approximately 50% of the classroom walkthroughs (scores 3–4) documented students solving a teacher-directed problem with or without collaboration involving one or more complex thinking processes (e.g., problem solving, decision making, inductive/deductive reasoning). Twenty-eight percent of the walkthroughs (scores 1–2) revealed that students were reporting back information with or without collaboration within a teacher-directed learning environment. Figure 9.3 reveals that approximately 63% of technology use (scores 1–3) was either (a) nonexistent, (b) used only by the teacher, or (c) used as an add-on and not needed for task completion.

Based on this data, the campus leadership team might want to investigate why the preponderance of teacher-centered classrooms and low level technology use persists on their campus, especially if the campus already emphasizes project-based learning and possesses an abundance of digital tools and environmental resources (e.g., high-access campus) for student collaboration.

Figure 9.2   Engaged Learning

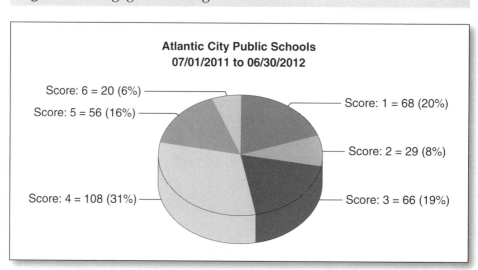

Figure 9.3 Technology Use

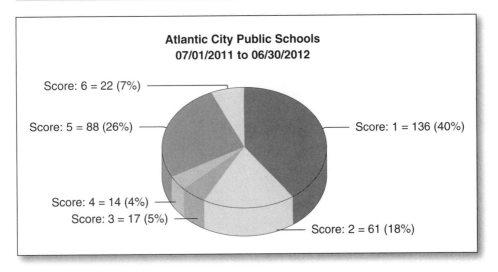

Atlantic City Public Schools
07/01/2011 to 06/30/2012

Score: 6 = 22 (7%)
Score: 5 = 88 (26%)
Score: 4 = 14 (4%)
Score: 3 = 17 (5%)
Score: 1 = 136 (40%)
Score: 2 = 61 (18%)

Step 5: Group Action Plan

Based on Figures 9.2 and 9.3, the campus leadership team might also conclude that, though professional development efforts have addressed project-based learning and the integration of technology, the actual implementation at the operational curriculum level reveals a reverse trend in favor of conventional instruction with little opportunity for student input using the available digital assets—two pillars of 21st Century Skills.

This awareness may lead to changes in existing professional development interventions. Possible suggestions might include a movement toward peer observations and a refocus on differentiated coaching techniques that address the individual informational needs and concerns of the teacher (e.g., proof that the changes are better than the present, implementation mechanics, the impact on individual students) (Kise, 2006).

The adage, "What gets measured, gets done," is a cornerstone of the Classroom Walkthrough with H.E.A.R.T. protocol used in the ACBOE. However, simply measuring what is happening in the classroom without a targeted focus or timely feedback can accomplish little toward instructional improvement. According to Gill (2010), "The problem is (often) the lack of will to use data to continuously improve systems and the lack of a process to interpret and apply data for continuous improvement" (para. 2).

Providing a set of walkthrough look-fors that offer a tangible way of creating both an individual teacher and a campus-wide snapshot coupled with ongoing dialogue served as a valuable resource in the ACBOE to promote student academic success, reflective practice in the classroom, and, ultimately, a 21st Century learning environment system-wide.

Figure 9.4 displays teacher feedback regarding their participation in the H.E.A.R.T. Walkthrough process in the ACBOE. Two critical columns, Columns E and G, reveal two central goals of the walkthrough process: to ensure that (1) administrators provide face-to-face feedback and (2) teachers view the feedback as conducive to their professional growth.

Based on the April 2012 report, 81% of the staff reported that their administrator met with them after the walkthrough to provide feedback and 92% of the staff reported that the feedback was a useful part of their continuous improvement process. These percentages closely approximate the ACBOE's annual goal of 90/90 whereby 90% of the staff report receiving feedback and 90% perceive the feedback as beneficial.

However, the key to the success of the H.E.A.R.T. Walkthrough process occurred behind the scenes far removed from the classroom. The ACBOE administration took every precaution to ensure that the walkthrough protocol was viewed as a professional development opportunity unrelated to the teacher evaluation process. District administrators met with teacher union officials throughout the entire adoption period of the H.E.A.R.T. Walkthrough program to achieve this goal. To date, no union grievance has been filed by staff members in the district who view the H.E.A.R.T. Walkthrough protocol exclusively as an informal professional development intervention unrelated to the requirements of the teacher evaluation process.

Professional Development

The ACBOE has invested heavily over the years in professional development opportunities for the district's rank and file, offering a combination of online, blended, and onsite courses, workshops, and summer institutes consistent with the tenets of Digital Age Best Practices. As noted earlier in this chapter, Figure 9.1 provides a graphic illustration of the alignment of Digital Age Best Practices to Moersch's original H.E.A.T. Framework, which later morphed into the district's H.E.A.R.T. look-fors, with the addition of rubric design. The ACBOE currently offers all staff members in the district individual online or blended asynchronous courses addressing each of the H.E.A.R.T. components (i.e., High Level Thinking Processes, Engaging Students,

Figure 9.4 ACBOE Teacher Feedback

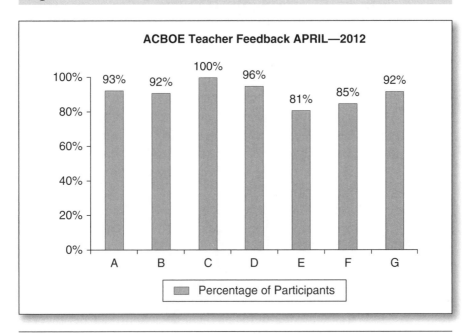

Figure 9.4 displays teacher feedback to the Classroom Walkthrough with H.E.A.R.T. process for April 2012 based on survey data collected from *71% of teachers experiencing a classroom walk through* during April 2012 in the Atlantic City Board of Education.

Graph legend

A = Teachers reported receiving a H.E.A.R.T. Walkthrough report.

B = Teachers acknowledged that a summary of their lesson was included in the H.E.A.R.T. Walkthrough report.

C = Teachers reported receiving at least one commendation about their lesson.

D = Teachers reported receiving at least one recommendation about their lesson.

E = Teachers reported that their administrative team met with them to provide feedback.

F = Teachers acknowledged receiving their feedback within one week of their classroom walkthrough.

G = Teachers reported the administrative feedback received was a useful part of the continuous improvement process (e.g., positive, productive, promotes reflective practice).

Authentic Connection, Rubric Design, and Technology Use). Additional courseware supporting targeted district initiatives, including the 5E Instructional Model for Lesson Planning, Differentiated Instruction, and Informal Assessment, have been created to provide staff twenty-four/seven access to the skills, resources, and strategies to elevate the amount of student H.E.A.R.T. in the classroom and support the tenets of Digital Age Best Practices.

External incentives, including staff development credit hours for district-approved professional development and reimbursement for district-approved university graduate courses, provide further impetus for staff to seek continuous growth opportunities aligned to the district's vision for teaching and learning. Internal personnel investments involving the employment of a cadre of math and reading coaches has provided classroom teachers with the needed resources and job-embedded modeling to elevate the fidelity of district-adopted initiatives ranging from the math benchmarking process to the literacy collaborative.

Districtwide Articulation

Implementing several initiatives in a relative brief time period can create perceived confusion and passive resistance among key stakeholders, even with the best of intentions. As Peter Senge reminds us, "People don't resist change. They resist being changed." Though pedagogically sound and research based, the amount of change introduced into the instructional curriculum within the ACBOE from an outsider's perspective may have appeared overwhelming. A comprehensive literacy initiative (Literacy Collaborative) coupled with a new math benchmarking process, classroom walkthrough protocol (H.E.A.R.T. Walkthroughs), and lesson planning format (5E Model) could have produced a negative backlash; yet, the district's focus on strategic articulation practices at the district and campus level provided staff with viable outlets to become empowered in the change process.

At the district level, bimonthly administrator meetings were implemented to address building personnel issues, ensure that pacing of the literacy and math curricula were consistent across the district, and receive first-hand updates on new policies affecting stakeholders. For example, concerns with the H.E.A.R.T. Walkthrough process lead to the creation of both an online and onsite professional development course for administrators. Additionally, the district contracted services from outside experts to assist campus administrators monthly with the walkthrough process in an attempt to increase the inter-rater reliability of these informal classroom visitations.

At the campus level, careful vigilance to the perceptions of students, parents, and staff involving teaching and learning practices, organizational structures, and interpersonal relationships resulted in an annual school climate needs assessment. Each campus in the ACBOE administered the School Climate Inventory to gauge faculty and staff perceptions of different areas related to school climate. Systematic collection and reporting of this school-based data enabled school building leaders to assess perceptions and opinions of school personnel and develop strategies to address climate factors that may inhibit or limit school effectiveness. The School Climate Inventory used in the ACBOE consists of seven dimensions or scales logically and empirically linked with factors associated with effective school organizational climates. The seven dimensions appear as Figure 9.5.

Figure 9.5 Seven Dimensions

The seven dimensions of the inventory are the following:

Collaboration. The extent to which the administration, faculty, and students cooperate and participate in problem solving.

Environment. The extent to which positive learning environments exist.

Expectations. The extent to which students are expected to learn and be responsible.

Instruction. The extent to which the instructional program is well developed and implemented.

Involvement. The extent to which parents and the community are involved in the school.

Leadership. The extent to which the administration provides instructional leadership.

Order. The extent to which the environment is ordered and appropriate student behaviors are present.

The ACBOE experience mirrors the ongoing change efforts of similar urban school systems entrenched in a myriad of social, cultural, and academic challenges among stakeholders. Yet, it was the baseline stakeholders themselves (students, parents, faculty), who came together through parent/teacher conferences, professional learning communities, school in-services, and campus school-site council meetings to execute the change process, that produced an increased sense of urgency and a heightened level of fidelity to each change effort and, in turn, opened the door to a full-scale implementation of many of the Digital Age Best Practices.

SECTION III

Implementation Plan

Full-scale execution of the Digital Age Best Practices at a high level of fidelity does not occur overnight. As with any change effort, the process may appear somewhat slow and fragmented. Change is an ongoing process as well as a common thread that runs through all school systems regardless of size, grade level, or setting. Section III focuses on the key processes and strategies for achieving sustainability with the Digital Age Best Practices. As a highly personal process, change requires constant vigilance to an individual's or group's perceptions, feelings, and actions. Figure E provides a useful depiction of the change process applied to a new campus initiative (i.e., new teacher evaluation program). The reactions often mirror stages of emotions that one cycles through during a period of significant change or upheaval. The graph in Figure E is based on a model originally developed in the 1960s by Elisabeth Kübler-Ross to explain the grieving process. Since it has been used extensively to help individuals understand their reactions to sudden change in many fields, I use it here to illustrate its utility when applied to a new innovation on campus.

Whether the person is riding the emotional roller coaster over a new district policy or the transfer to another school, understanding the dynamics of the change process illustrated in Figure E is critical to planning meaningful professional development. Moving individuals within a school system from initial shock to final acceptance

Figure E   Kübler-Ross Model Applied to New Teacher Evaluation

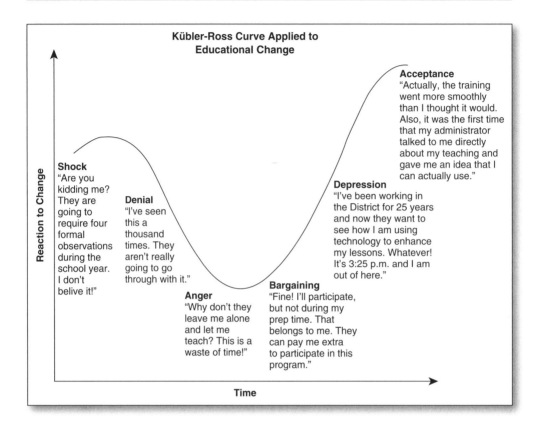

requires careful consideration of the effect of the change effort on all key stakeholders, including students, teachers, building/district administration, and the broader community. The focus on personal concerns in the change process is perhaps best documented in Hord et al. (1987) Concerns-Based Adoption Model (CBAM) featuring two separate constructs: Stages of Concern (Figure F) and Level of Use (Figure G).

What types of professional development do you offer stakeholders who are at the anger stage versus those who have progressed to the acceptance level? The Levels of Use (LoU) and Stages of Concern (SoC) frameworks can help guide school leaders as they move individuals within their organization from Non-use (Level 0) to Renewal (Level 6). In the ACBOE, the target goal was the Routine stage of the LoU Framework relating to implementing several Digital Age Best Practices manifested in content benchmarking, differentiated instruction, and technology integration. Chapter 10 discusses strategies for differentiating professional development based in part of the LoU and SoC frameworks.

Figure F　Stages of Concern

Stage of Concern	Expression of Concern
6. Refocusing	I have some ideas about something that would work even better.
5. Collaboration	How can I relate what I am doing to what others are doing?
4. Consequence	How is my use affecting learners? How can I refine it to have more impact?
3. Management	I seem to be spending all my time getting materials ready.
2. Personal	How will using it affect me?
1. Informational	I would like to know more about it.
0. Awareness	I am not concerned about it.

Source: Hall and Hord (2000)

Figure G　Levels of Use

Level of Use	Behavioral Indicator of Level
VI. Renewal	The user is seeking more effective alternatives to the established use of the innovation.
V. Integration	The user is making deliberate efforts to coordinate with others in using the innovation.
IVB. Refinement	The user is making changes to increase outcomes.
IVA.	The user is making few or no changes and has an established pattern of use.
III. Mechanical	The user is making changes to better organize use of the innovation.
II. Preparation	The user has definite plans to begin using the innovation.
I. Orientation	The user is taking the initiative to learn more about the innovation.
0. Non-Use	The user has no interest, is taking no action.

Source: Hall and Hord (2000)

To date, the ACBOE has followed indirectly a three-stage process for achieving long-term change: Building Capacity, Implementing Change, and Sustaining Independence. Each stage along with the accompanying checklist are described in Chapter 11. Chapter 11 addresses each of these stages. Stage 1, Building Capacity, builds the pedagogical capacity focusing on H.E.A.T. or H.E.A.R.T., content benchmarking, and using the existing digital tools and enhanced resources to promote the change process. Stage 2, Implementing Change, involves full-scale implementation of H.E.A.T. or H.E.A.R.T., classroom walkthroughs, and collaborative learning environments with special emphasis on differentiated instruction. Stage 3, Sustaining Independence, focuses on designing 21st century assessments, expanding teachers' repertoire of instructional strategies, and refining a sustainable cycle of continuous improvement. The reader should note that this three-stage model does not represent a three-year implementation process. Some schools are able to move from Stage 1, Building Capacity to Stage 3, Sustaining Independence within a single school year, whereas another school system may remain at Building Capacity for several years.

The success in the ACBOE in moving from Stage 1 to Stage 3 with many of the Digital Age Best Practices was the result of proactive leadership, a plethora of dedicated staff members, and the support of key stakeholders within the broader Atlantic City community.

10

Differentiated Professional Development

How often has the following scenario occurred in your professional career: A new program (e.g., 1:1 initiative, new math program, differentiated instruction) is first introduced to your campus staff followed by intensive staff development (i.e., online, onsite, blended). The participating teachers rave about their staff development experiences and remark with enthusiasm how the new program will improve student achievement, elevate the level of teaching innovation, prepare students for a digital world, and/or improve the efficiency of their daily routines. As you and your colleagues visit classrooms "integrating" the new program a month later, you are bewildered by either a low fidelity of implementation or no implementation at all.

What happened? How can educators who, on one hand, laud the efforts of their staff development colleagues as well as the innovation itself during training sessions yet put forth limited or no effort with the actual implementation? Why do endless hours of professional development often fail to translate into any appreciable change in classroom practices and routines? According to Kise (2006), "Asking teachers to change their practices often means asking them to do things that sound absolutely hostile to them" (p. 10).

A general consensus within the research community has noted that individuals possess a unique belief structure that, in turn, influences personal action resulting in the formation of routines (Costa & Garmston, 1994; Duffy, 2003; Pohan & Aguilar, 2001). According to Pohan and Aguilar (2001), "teachers' beliefs serve as filters for their knowledge bases and will ultimately affect their actions" (p. 160).

Staff development attempts often fail because of (a) a lack of congruency with the individual teachers' belief structure and/or (b) a misguided focus of the change process directed at the innovation rather than the individual. Advocating the need for "teacher-centered" staff development, Kise advances four broad questions that should be considered as we plan professional development interventions:

1. What are the teacher's beliefs about how students learn?

2. How tightly are teachers' beliefs tied to their own strengths?

3. What are the teachers' beliefs about their roles in student success?

4. What else keeps teachers from trying new practices?

The first three questions address the need for a "common framework" in which to address the core beliefs of the individual as well as identify the role of the staff development professional in the change process. Focusing on a common framework provides a "level playing field" in which to diagnose the personality profile or learning style of individual teachers, leading to subsequent adjustments to the professional development intervention as well as changes in the role of the professional development facilitator. According to Kise, knowing your personality type gives you a window into understanding your learning style (2006). Once a personality type is identified, the staff development practitioner can then determine their role in the professional development intervention (e.g., trainer as expert, trainer as resource dispenser, trainer as trusted colleague), which leads to greater efficacy and, ultimately, increased fidelity involving the change effort.

Several years ago, I facilitated a teacher workshop on learning styles in the classroom. As an experiment, I grouped participants based on the outcome of their interaction with the Gregorc 4-Quadrant Model. Afterwards, I assigned a task (e.g., analyzing and adjusting the level of engagement of a middle school math lesson) that required group consensus. The concrete-sequential cluster of teachers quickly organized their efforts, articulated verbally the steps necessary to complete the assignment, and finished the task well before the first morning break. During this same time period, the abstract random group was still negotiating task responsibilities without any progress toward task completion.

What implications does this experiment have for professional development planners who attempt to leverage existing resources (e.g., time, funding, instructional and technological infrastructures) to promote the change process at the campus level? My role as the professional development facilitator needed to change based on the learning or thinking styles profile of the audience. A summary of the Gregorc 4-Quadrant Model applied to my learning styles workshop appears below.

Concrete Sequential. These participants tend to be grounded in reality and possess a propensity for information in an ordered, sequential, linear manner. Providing participants with an advanced organizer, lesson plan templates, and a specific timeline helped augment their completion of the task. For these individuals, my role was a well-equipped resource dispenser.

Concrete Random. These individuals are natural experimenters. Similar to the concrete sequential group, distributing advanced organizers and a timeline were helpful, but providing them with latitude to explore and discuss a multitude of options relating to the lesson plan modification was pivotal. My role in the staff development session for these individuals switched from resource dispenser to co-facilitator.

Abstract Random. These participants organize information through reflection and thrive in unstructured, people-oriented environments. Providing latitude for these individuals to create their own timeline and achieve group consensus relating to final outcomes was essential for their "success." For these individuals, my role was that of a trusted colleague, enabling me to enter their inner circle and help guide their progress.

Abstract Sequential. These individuals flourish within an environment that promotes theory and abstract thought. Supplying this group with an online option using a content management system, such as Moodle or Blackboard to investigate key theories about student engagement but with defined checkpoints for completion, enabled them to reflect on the content under investigation while providing a sense of accountability for project completion.

In attempting to diagnose the personality, learning style, or thinking style profile of individual teachers, there is no one "correct" assessment tool to use in your diagnosis. A plethora of personal profile inventories (e.g., Gregorc 4-Quadrant Model, Hemispheric Dominance Inventory Test) exist on the web that can help differentiate the content as well as the role of the staff development facilitator in the change process.

As one investigates these different personal profile inventory assessments, it is worth noting the subtle differences among the types of instruments. A personality profile is a test or inventory that measures how an individual interacts with others, communicates, makes decisions, and/or responds to stressful situations. A learning style profile is similar to a personality profile but focuses on an individual's preferred method of interacting with, taking in, and processing information.

Besides adjusting one's role in the staff development intervention to align with the dominant personality or learning profile of participants, what other variables prevent teachers from implementing new practices based on their professional learning experiences? Change is a highly personal and incremental experience. Smith (2010) outlines certain truisms about the change process:

- The greater the unpredictability, the greater the need for communication
- The greater the amount of participation, the greater the probability that issues and potential problems will be raised
- The greater the amount of time involved, the greater the level of participation
- The greater the number of problems identified early in the change process, the less the probability of error
- The greater the probability of success felt by the members of the organization, the greater the commitment to the change process
- The greater the commitment to the change process held by individuals in the organization, the greater their efforts will be directed toward making the change succeed
- The greater the ownership of the change process, the less resistance to the change

As mentioned earlier, a misguided focus of the change process directed at the innovation rather than the individual during staff development sessions can often lead to unsuccessful change efforts. Let's explore a case study involving the introduction of a 1:1 mobile device initiative at a middle school.

Middle School Case Study

Through a state grant, Serra Middle School received funding for 750 mobile devices involving Grades 6 through 8 over a three-year implementation period. The focus of the grant was to provide student access to mobile devices twenty-four/seven as part of the campus' transition into a "21st century" learning environment. The professional development consisted of a five-day summer technology camp attended by the Year 1 cohort teachers (sixth grade) followed by six full days of staff development during the academic year.

The summer professional development modeled teaching best-practices within a 1:1 learning environment, introduced teachers to a variety of Web 2.0 tools and resources, provided time for teachers to create sample lesson plans based on their content areas, and showcased the capabilities of mobile device technology. The summer session culminated with each teacher presenting a mini-lesson focusing on a particular content standard to his or her colleagues within a high access environment.

The staff development days during the academic year concentrated on specific implementation strategies, including job-embedded modeling of mobile device use within large groups, small groups, and center/stations as well as peer observations devoted to improving mobile device use in the classroom through collegial feedback. Grant participants were administered a pre/post assessment based on the LoTi Framework to ascertain growth in digital-age teaching and learning resulting from the 1:1 mobile device initiative. Results of the pre/post assessment are highlighted in Figures 10.0 and 10.1.

The results showed a slight decrease in the overall LoTi levels from the fall (Figure 10.0) through the spring semester (Figure 10.1). The predominant LoTi level remained at a LoTi Level 2 throughout the school year.

Why the lack of progress with the mobile device initiative at Sierra Middle School? The staff development targeted the essentials for a successful implementation—peer observations, job-embedded modeling, planning time to design lessons, and exploration of Web 2.0

Figure 10.0   Sierra Middle School Pre-Assessment LoTi Results

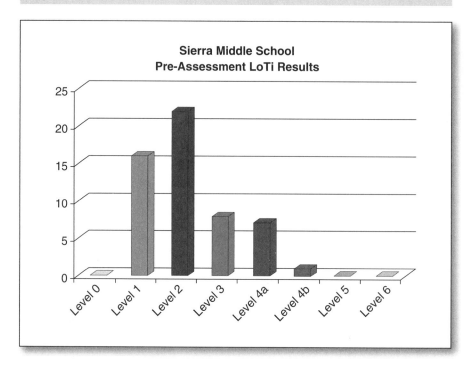

Figure 10.1   Sierra Middle School Post-Assessment LoTi Results

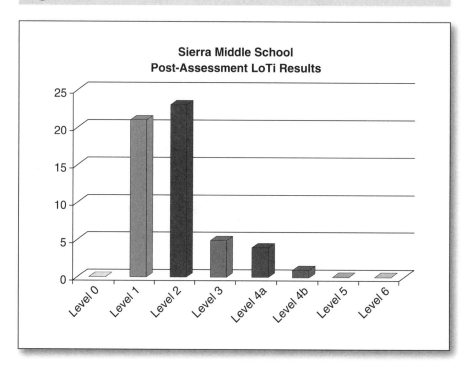

tools and resources. Yet, the results showed no significant movement in the manner in which the mobile devices were used throughout the school year.

A possible culprit could have been a misguided focus on the innovation (1:1 initiative) rather than on the individual teachers. Though staff development efforts addressed critical implementation barriers (e.g., unfamiliarity with the hardware, lack of time to pursue lesson planning), the concerns of the teachers may have not been adequately addressed. Based on the Stages of Concern framework (see Figure F), these concerns could have ranged from some teacher's need for more information about the innovation to other teachers' concerns about the impact of the innovation on student achievement.

Failing to address the core concerns of the teachers may have seriously diminished individual teachers' commitment to the change process. Though staff development interventions were frequent and consistent with best practices tied to the innovation (e.g., 1:1 initiative), the lack of attention devoted to the concerns of the classroom practitioners implementing the 1:1 initiative in their classrooms may have compromised implementation efforts.

Addressing the needs of individual teachers as they relate to planning professional development (e.g., identifying the personality or learning profile of the participants) and monitoring program implementation (identifying the current concerns of individual teachers) are critical steps to the change process. The success of any change effort may, therefore, be directly proportional to the amount of quality time allocated initially for adjusting or differentiating the content, delivery, and follow-up of the professional development along with defining the role of the professional development professional. Bowgren and Sever (2010) offer a practical three-step model for differentiating staff development based on the *I Do, We Do, You Do* process as summarized below:

Step 1: Teacher leaders and facilitators introduce and demonstrate new strategies.

Step 2: Teacher leaders and facilitators determine the needs of each teacher and provide the appropriate types of support, such as coaching, workshops, or co-teaching.

Step 3: Teachers are ready to use the strategies independently in the classroom.

In the ACBOE, the use of strategies to differentiate professional development opportunities based on staff emotional levels, modality strengths, or even stages of concern is in the beginning stage at best. Given the myriad of programs implemented annually, the ability to create individualized professional development plans based on these variables remains a long range goal.

However, efforts have been made in the district to promote both flexible and targeted professional development. As mentioned earlier, the district has already created online courses for several district initiatives (e.g., 5E Model, H.E.A.R.T.) that provide staff with flexibility for exploring key math and literacy concepts and strategies asynchronously. The employment of both math and literacy coaches has provided differentiated interventions for staff members in the form of job-embedded modeling, peer coaching, and lesson planning.

Given the mounting pressures to prepare students for a digitally charged world, promote greater rigor and relevance in the classroom, and ensure student success on high stakes measures, the need to promote more strategic planning to the change process relating to differentiating all aspects of staff development is essential. The successful implementation of the Digital Age Best Practices into any learning community is no exception. The emergence of the SoC/LoU frameworks onto the educational landscape occurred several decades ago, yet, their relevancy to the successful execution of the change process is as relevant today.

SUMMARY

Whereas Chapter 10 addressed the microcosmic nature of the change process involving the individual, Chapter 11 will delve into the macro level of organizational change relating to Digital Age Best Practices. As we explore organizational change, consider the following questions:

- What organizational processes are necessary to ensure long-term sustainability of any change effort?
- How much leeway to the fidelity of the change effort is considered acceptable?
- What happens to the change effort when new leadership (e.g., new superintendent, new principal) enters the picture?

11

Three-Stage Model

The ACBOE instituted a de facto change model to guide many of their actions impacting curriculum decision making at the institutional, instructional, and operational levels. This chapter encapsulates the district's collective decision making relating to school improvement, including the implementation of the Digital Age Best Practices into three successive stages: Building Capacity, Implementing Change, Sustaining Independence.

Building Capacity

Building Capacity establishes the foundation for change. This stage focuses on understanding the obstacles that inhibit stakeholders from realizing their instructional or organizational goals while enhancing their abilities through strategically placed professional development. The goal of building capacity is to address potential problems before they arise and threaten the entire change process while considering the needs of individual staff members. Stage 1, Building Capacity, requires the development of conditions that allow stakeholders to build and enhance existing knowledge and skills. Critical steps in the Building Capacity process include the following:

- Developing a conceptual framework
- Developing a vision and strategy
- Acquiring skills and resources

Developing a conceptual framework involves a four-phase cyclical process, including assess, plan, implement, and sustain. This cyclical process guides the entire decision-making process impacting classroom pedagogy at the operational curriculum level. At the conclusion of the Building Capacity stage, a school entity would have developed a vision and an accompanying strategy for the change effort, including the creation of

- campus expectations aligned with H.E.A.T. or H.E.A.R.T.,
- staff routines for continuous improvement through targeted professional development,
- a Next Steps Plan aligned with targeted campus academic goals, and
- a structured sequence of data collection (e.g., state assessment scores, content benchmarking data).

Figure 11.0 offers a generic checklist for school leaders contemplating a structured sequence to the change process impacting student achievement and teaching and learning.

Figure 11.0 Building Capacity

Assess

❏ Complete self-assessment questionnaire to ascertain professional development needs of targeted staff members at participating campus.
❏ Conduct pre-assessment data gathering in each targeted staff member's classroom relating to dominant instructional methodologies used.
❏ Assess benchmarking process to ascertain the presence of four specific criteria: (1) possesses the look and feel of the actual statewide assessment, (2) measures what has already been taught, (3) ensures an efficient turn-around time for data analysis and summary, and (4) provides follow-up interventions for students at a LoTi 3+.

Plan

❏ Conduct a review of most recent state assessment data with curriculum specialist/building administration and staff members; review testing schedule and address potential gaps.
❏ Develop Next Steps Plan for campus focusing on SMART (Specific, Measurable, Attainable, Realistic, Timely) Goals and

deliverables for the following indicators: H.E.A.T. (Higher-Order Thinking, Engaged Learning, Authentic Connections, Technology Use) and statewide assessment results.

☐ Ensure that all building administrators are proficient in the five-step classroom walkthrough with H.E.A.T. protocol and Digital Age Best Practices.

Implement

☐ Provide resource sharing sessions for targeted staff members focusing on the elements of H.E.A.T.

☐ Conduct H.E.A.T. orientation session for staff prior to the start of the academic year.

☐ Retrofit campus grade benchmark assessment interventions for each tested content area so that they meet the expectations of a LoTi 3+.

☐ Provide ongoing blended professional development interventions for targeted staff members focusing on retrofitting the elements of H.E.A.T. within the staff's rhythm of instruction and classroom routines.

☐ Provide ongoing in-class modeling and peer mentoring of targeted staff members throughout the school year.

☐ Focus on peer H.E.A.T. observations and LoTi lesson makeovers during the first semester.

☐ Focus on classroom walkthroughs with emphasis on the key H.E.A.T. look-fors during the second semester.

☐ Enable targeted staff members to enroll in professional development day-equivalent online courses addressing the components of H.E.A.T.

Sustain

☐ Provide monthly monitoring of all target staff members' H.E.A.T. Walkthroughs at the building and district levels beginning at the second semester.

☐ Review benchmarking results quarterly, making adjustments and creating additional student interventions, if necessary, based on the data.

☐ Conduct post-assessment data gathering in each targeted staff member's classroom in the spring relating to dominant instructional methodologies used.

☐ Prepare annual evaluation report.

Implementation Challenges

Ensuring that all key stakeholders have embraced a common vision for success is vital to the completion of the Building Capacity stage in a timely fashion. One group of stakeholders often overlooked is board members. Recognizing how one or two new board members can easily shift the dynamics of the board and, ultimately, the policy making of the school system is crucial. Continually articulating how the change efforts are in the best interest of students (a) at community events and board meetings; (b) in district and building newsletters, radio interviews, and blog posts; and (c) during informal gatherings can help re-energize all stakeholders (e.g., teachers, parents, board members).

For the ACBOE, ensuring a high degree of teacher efficacy was essential to the change process. Moving staff members to different grade levels based on their areas of strengths, garnering grass-roots support for the critical Digital Age Best Practices, and allowing more flexibility for campus librarians to work directly with teachers were but a few of the strategies used by district leadership to lay the foundation for change.

Implementing Change

Stage 2, Implementing Change, provides each campus with the mechanism to transform theory into full-scale practice, and it provides a realistic check as to the fidelity of full-scale implementation of one or more of the Digital Age Best Practices. This stage enables key stakeholders to monitor the change effort over time and make adjustments as necessary while addressing potential problems and proactively addressing them. Figure 11.1 offers a generic checklist for school leaders executing the Implementing Change stage. As with the Building Capacity stage, Implementing Change requires commitment from all key stakeholders to the campus SMART goals defined by the Next Steps Plan.

Implementation Challenges

Full-scale implementation of any change initiative, such as the Digital Age Best Practices, can create pressure points among key stakeholders that too often result in passive resistance, union grievances, morale issues, and, in some instances, outwardly defiant behavior. In the ACBOE, district leadership prevented many of these signs of low-level implementation by (a) establishing a proactive relationship with the teacher's union and (b) empowering school building leaders.

Figure 11.1   Implementing Change

Assess

☐ Complete self-assessment questionnaire to ascertain professional development needs of targeted staff members at participating campus.

☐ Conduct pre-assessment data gathering in each targeted staff member's classroom relating to dominant instructional methodologies used.

Plan

☐ Conduct a review of prior-year's state assessment data with curriculum specialist/building administration and staff members; review testing schedule and address potential gaps.

☐ Revise Next Steps Plan based on the statewide assessment results and staff instructional practices data.

☐ Develop individualized professional development plans for targeted staff members based on the results of the teacher self-assessment.

Implement

☐ Provide resource-sharing sessions for targeted staff members focusing on one or more Digital Age Best Practice.

☐ Ensure that campus grade benchmark assessment interventions for each tested content area are at a LoTi 3+.

☐ Provide ongoing blended professional development interventions for targeted staff members based on the revised Next Steps Plan.

☐ Provide targeted staff members opportunities for peer mentoring and co-teaching at the impacted grade levels/content areas.

☐ Focus the peer observation and the professional learning community process on one or more Digital Age Best Practice.

☐ Refine H.E.A.T. Walkthrough protocols with emphasis on the connection between pedagogical decisions and the linkage to specific curricular content and the Digital Age Best Practices.

☐ Enable targeted staff members to enroll in professional development day-equivalent online courses addressing one or more Digital Age Best Practices.

Sustain

☐ Provide monthly monitoring of all target staff members' H.E.A.T. Walkthroughs at the building and district levels.

☐ Review benchmarking results quarterly, making adjustments and creating additional student interventions, if necessary, based on the data.

☐ Conduct post-assessment data gathering in each targeted staff member's classroom in the spring relating to dominant instructional methodologies used.

☐ Prepare annual LoTi Evaluation Report.

District officials kept the teacher's union in the loop on all instructional initiatives, including the adoption of the online lesson planner integrating the 5E Model, H.E.A.R.T. classroom walkthroughs, and the teacher evaluation system. This approach helped to minimize any adverse effect resulting from changes impacting the sanctity of a teacher's instructional curriculum. The theme of proactive leadership also applied to school leaders. A major goal of the ACBOE was to ensure a heightened sense of transparency involving instructional decisions made at the district level. To this end, bimonthly district-wide leadership meetings were formed that provided greater opportunity for building level input into the instructional decision-making process.

A key component of Stage 2, Implementing Change, was the full-scale implementation of the H.E.A.R.T. classroom walkthrough process. This strategy enabled school building leaders to gauge accurately the level of implementation of targeted Digital Age Best Practices as well as provide assistance to teachers on an individual basis.

Sustaining Independence

Why do change efforts fail? According to most publications, the mortality rate of any change effort fluctuates somewhere between 65% and 75%. In baseball, this percentage of batting failure would earn you a seven figure salary; in organizations, this failure rate often cripples the growth of an entity, decreases morale, and worse yet, increases staff skepticism about the change process in general. The reasons for these failed change attempts can be lumped into four broad categories:

- Poor communication
- Lack of top level commitment
- Unfocused or half-hearted efforts
- Poor planning

What happens to most innovations once the funding runs out? All too frequently, the innovation dies because critical support mechanisms are no longer in place to sustain the change effort. Grant-funded consultants and staff so vital to the change process disappear, summer institutes that once promoted synergy and esprit de corp among content area teachers vanish, and accountability monitoring measures become relegated to the back burner.

As a component of the change process, Sustaining Independence is pivotal. Figure 11.2 provides a checklist of the Sustaining Independence stage of the change process.

Figure 11.2 Sustaining Independence

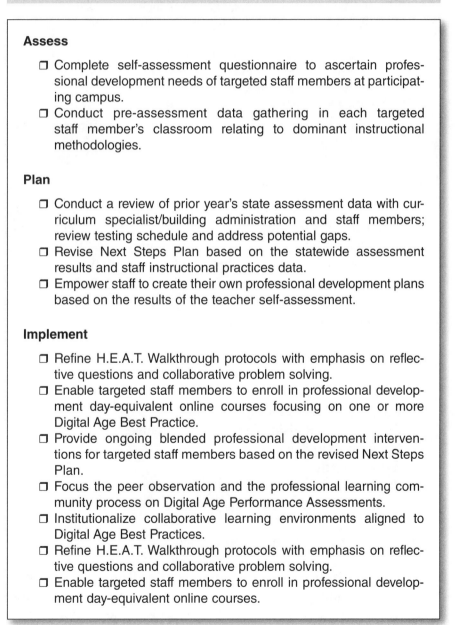

Assess

☐ Complete self-assessment questionnaire to ascertain professional development needs of targeted staff members at participating campus.
☐ Conduct pre-assessment data gathering in each targeted staff member's classroom relating to dominant instructional methodologies.

Plan

☐ Conduct a review of prior year's state assessment data with curriculum specialist/building administration and staff members; review testing schedule and address potential gaps.
☐ Revise Next Steps Plan based on the statewide assessment results and staff instructional practices data.
☐ Empower staff to create their own professional development plans based on the results of the teacher self-assessment.

Implement

☐ Refine H.E.A.T. Walkthrough protocols with emphasis on reflective questions and collaborative problem solving.
☐ Enable targeted staff members to enroll in professional development day-equivalent online courses focusing on one or more Digital Age Best Practice.
☐ Provide ongoing blended professional development interventions for targeted staff members based on the revised Next Steps Plan.
☐ Focus the peer observation and the professional learning community process on Digital Age Performance Assessments.
☐ Institutionalize collaborative learning environments aligned to Digital Age Best Practices.
☐ Refine H.E.A.T. Walkthrough protocols with emphasis on reflective questions and collaborative problem solving.
☐ Enable targeted staff members to enroll in professional development day-equivalent online courses.

(Continued)

Figure 11.2 (Continued)

Sustain

❏ Provide quarterly monitoring of all target staff members' H.E.A.T. Walkthroughs at the building and district levels.

❏ Review benchmarking results quarterly, making adjustments and creating additional student interventions, if necessary, based on the data.

❏ Conduct post-assessment data gathering in each targeted staff member's classroom in the Spring relating to dominant instructional methodologies used.

❏ Prepare annual LoTi Evaluation Report.

Implementation Challenges

One of the keys to sustaining change in the ACBOE was the ongoing monitoring of multiple change efforts (e.g., content benchmarking, 5E Model, H.E.A.R.T.). The use of the H.E.A.R.T. Walkthrough protocol was a key ingredient in this process to ensure that the critical elements of the change effort did not disappear. Stanleigh (2008) offers a crisp summary of measures that should be considered to sustain any change process including

- Accept that change is a process.
- Move forward step-by-step.
- Assess potential risks and generate motivation.
- Form a powerful guiding coalition.
- Create a shared vision for corporate change.
- Communicate that vision.
- Empower others to act on the vision.
- Plan for and create short-term wins.
- Consolidate improvement and keep the momentum for change moving.
- Institutionalize the new approaches.

Many of the above measures represent proven, time-honored postulates for sustaining organizational change. However, a few of these measures are sometimes beyond the control of the school system. When new leadership enters the picture (e.g., new board members, superintendent, principal), the philosophy of "out with the old, in with the new" sometimes dominates the new educational landscape. The old vision is replaced with a new approach that may or may not possess the salient characteristics of the previous change effort.

SUMMARY

In the ACBOE, this was not the case. The stability of top-level leadership enabled each change effort relating to Digital Age Best Practices to occur incrementally and organically while becoming a fixed component in the culture of each school building. As the reader will learn in Section IV, sustaining educational change requires more than longevity on the job as an instructional leader. It also requires a strict adherence to the 5Cs of leadership: *Cultivation, Courage, Creativity, Commitment,* and *Communication.*

SECTION IV

Instructional Leadership

I n the 21st century the notion of instructional leadership has broadened to include stakeholders other than the traditional building principal. Given the mushrooming effect of new research and information about student learning that classroom teachers, coaches, and content supervisors possess, it would be misleading to assume that the building principal is the sole-source expert on curriculum and instruction, offering sage instructional advice to a group of pedagogical novices.

Similar to the changing role of the classroom teacher from *sage on the stage* to co-facilitator in the learning process, the concept of instructional leadership has broadened into a field of shared leadership among several stakeholders. This is not to diminish the role of the principal. The need for strong, focused leaders who can communicate and execute a vision for change that positively impacts all stakeholders and leads to increased student academic progress and improved teaching and learning is in high demand. The importance of teachers and administrators working together to shape a vision and execute a vision is paramount.

The National Association of Secondary School Principals (NASSP) outlines a specific set of skill dimensions required of a 21st Century principal in the areas of educational leadership, resolving complex problems, communication, and developing self and others. These leadership skills ranging from developing a vision and establishing clear goals to making high quality decisions based on the available evidence are some of the needed pre-requisite of today's instructional leaders. As a former co-director of a regional NASSP Assessment Center, I can attest to the integrity and reliability of the assessment process for targeting the necessary behaviors of aspiring administrators based on a set of research-based best practices.

Observing a group of aspiring administrators as they participated in a series of leaderless group simulations, prioritized sample in-basket action items such as an irate parent seated outside the principal's office, and worked collaboratively in constructing a mock board presentation while a group of practicing building and district administrators (i.e., evaluators) recorded their every word and gesture provided an opportunity to diagnose and prescribe specific professional development interventions that would help each administrative candidate succeed in an actual leadership position.

What is missing from this process that the NASSP defines as 21st century leadership is another set of best practices that reaches beyond the science and into the art of leadership. The art of leadership is manifested into a set of principles that have universal relevance regardless of position on the proverbial educational ladder but do separate great leaders from good leaders. Chapter 12 introduces these universal principles that I have coined, the 5Cs of Instructional Leadership.

12

5Cs of Instructional Leadership

Research abounds that references the pivotal role that building and district leaders play in the educational change process. Successful implementation of any district or school-based innovation can be traced to the attitude and actions of leadership. Whether the change involves the implementation of a new reading program, the creation of professional learning communities, or the introduction of a new way of conducting classroom walkthroughs, the behavior of district and campus leaders can bring either success or failure with any innovation.

In the ACBOE, many of these leadership postulates representing the 5C's of Instructional Leadership have been a vital part of the change process. The 5Cs of Instructional Leadership include *Cultivation*, *Courage*, *Creativity*, *Commitment*, and *Communication*. Each of these attributes continue to serve at the core of the ACBOE experience.

Cultivation

How many times have you heard someone describe their educational leader (e.g., superintendent, principal, director) as a true visionary—someone who is able to envision a bold plan to improve student achievement, reinvigorate a dormant curriculum, or create a 21st century learning environment, yet is unable to execute on that vision? Though creating a vision for instructional change or renewal at the campus or district level is laudable, the inability to cultivate that vision for success into a viable plan of action can lead to staff discontent, apathy, and worse yet, passive resistance to the entire change process. Campus and district leaders who are able to cultivate a climate of change against perceived environmental barriers (e.g., standardized tests, staff resistance) possess that intangible attribute of a true instructional leader that cannot be taught in a graduate course.

In the ACBOE, cultivating a vision of improved classroom instruction and increased student achievement did not happen immediately with the passage of a board resolution, faculty attendance at a summer workshop, or the execution of an isolated H.E.A.R.T. Walk-through. All of these events were symbiotically and tactically aligned to a larger vision that emphasized the tenets of Digital Age Best Practices. As the district moves forward, curriculum initiatives surrounding the Common Core State Standards as well as professional development addressing STEM (science, technology, engineering, mathematics) and teacher and principal evaluation systems will continue to use the elements of H.E.A.R.T. and Digital Age Best Practices as the litmus test to gauge their fidelity to the district's larger vision for continuous improvement.

Courage

Courage represents the ability to "stand for principle" in the face of mounting pressure to find quick-fix solutions (e.g., extensive test prep exercises, over-reliance on drill and practice activities) for long-term problems. In schools today, no one can escape the inevitable "high-stakes" test given each spring to measure what students know in targeted grade levels and content areas. The ability to challenge conventional wisdom and focus on what research as well as your "gut instincts" tell you works best for students academically (e.g., higher-order thinking, student engagement, authentic problem solving, differentiated instruction, cooperative learning) defines the Courage level of instructional leaders. Acting courageously simply means applying one's convictions to a problem or challenge regardless of outside pressures. Successful school systems who achieve their targeted goals are lead by leaders with courage.

During the 2012 through 2013 school year, the district adopted a customized but state-approved teacher and principal evaluation protocol aligned to H.E.A.R.T. and Digital Age Best Practices, even though 90% of the other school systems in the state were instituting a more conventional model. Rather then acquiescing to indirect pressure to follow the actions of neighboring school entities, the district opted to remain true to their convictions regarding the importance of H.E.A.R.T. to achieve the larger instructional outcomes—that is, improved instruction and increased student academic progress.

Creativity

Top-flight school and district leaders are able to exercise their creative instincts to find solutions to problems. Where others see barriers, they see opportunities. Think about those building administrators whom you have known personally, read about in a periodical, or viewed on YouTube who were able, in a relatively short period of time, to increase student attendance, reduce violence on campus, improve school climate for both staff and students, and raise test scores. Many of us have met these individuals and watched as they steered through obstacles and against overwhelming odds, with naysayers clamoring, It can't be done! These individuals are able to exercise their creativity with a large dosage of personal initiative and implement their vision for success.

Exercising the necessary creativity to secure teacher union support for the district-approved H.E.A.R.T. Walkthrough protocol was no small feat. Over a five-year period, zero union grievances have been filed by members of the teacher rank and file. Why? By strategically linking the H.E.A.R.T. Walkthrough to staff professional development planning and emphasizing the non-evaluative nature of the walkthrough process, the ACBOE administrative team was able to alleviate potential fears about the intent of the H.E.A.R.T. Walkthrough system. As mentioned earlier, the district was also able to implement a new lesson planning system (i.e., 5E Model) by strategically working with union representatives through the entire approval process.

Commitment

In the movie *The Patriot*, the oldest son, played by the late Heath Ledger, continually reminded his father to "stay the course" on the mission to defeat the British during the Revolutionary War rather than give up or focus energy on personal vendettas. Successful school and district leaders are able to stay committed to the implementation of their action plans even when the popular decision would be to acquiesce to special interest groups on campus or stop the process entirely. During my graduate years as an aspiring administrator at San Diego State University, I had a professor I will never forget. Dr. Al Moreno often kidded us about the definition of leadership, which he said was to "find which way the herd is going and get out in front." True leaders do not rely on Gallup Polls to do the right thing; they "just do it."

In the case of the ACBOE, securing a waiver to continue the highly successful math benchmarking protocol as opposed to adopting the state's recommended model curriculum attests to the district's courage to "stay the course." Though a majority of school systems readily adopted the state recommended curriculum, the district's focus on consistency and continuity with their existing benchmarking process outweighed the more popular option.

Communication

Effective communication is the cornerstone for an effective leader. Oftentimes, staff is unsure about the school's central mission when the level of communication from the principal is reduced to a weekly email or a brief speech during a faculty meeting or via the intercom. Quality communication extends beyond the spoken or printed word. Schools that achieve overwhelming success are lead by people who are able to translate their words into action and create a consensus among all key stakeholders as to the school's mission. Though the level of communication starts with the principal, it does not stop there. Quality communication involves all participants on campus best manifested in clusters of professional learning communities.

In the ACBOE, proactive and ongoing communication with board members, union representatives, department of education officials, and government leaders as well as with individual teachers helped to establish a climate of trust among all stakeholders. This trust factor has been pivotal in ensuring the rapid institutionalization of many district initiatives ranging from the H.E.A.R.T. Walkthrough protocol to the use of the 5E Model for lesson plan development.

SUMMARY

The 5 Cs of instructional leadership are central to the change process in any school system. According to Joiner, "effective change requires skilled leadership that can integrate the soft human elements with hard business actions" (Joiner, 1987). Successful school systems are led by individuals who possess these qualities.

In the case of the Atlantic City Board of Education, the presence of a stable and proactive leadership team that manifested most, if not all, of the 5Cs of Instructional Leadership enabled the district to achieve unprecedented success with its instructional curriculum. Similar to the Digital Age Best Practices, many of these leadership principles are familiar to most stakeholders, yet transforming simple rhetoric into action is what set apart the Atlantic City experience from other change efforts.

References

Ainsworth, L., & Viegut, D. (2006). *Common formative assessments: How to connect standards-based instruction and assessment.* Thousand Oaks, CA: Corwin.

Anderson, R. D. (2002). Reforming science teaching: What research says about inquiry. *Journal of Science Teacher Education, 13*(1), 1–12.

Archer, J. (1998). The link to higher test scores. *Education Week, 18*(5), 10–21.

Baker, E. L., Gearhart, M., & Herman, J. L. (1994). Evaluating the apple classrooms of tomorrow[SM]. In E. L. Baker & H. F. O'Neil Jr. (Eds.), *Technology assessment in education and training* (pp. 173–198). Hillsdale, NJ: Erlbaum.

Barrows, H. (2002). Is it truly possible to have such a thing as dPBL? *Distance Education, 23*(1), 119–122.

Black, P. J., & Wiliam, D. (1998a). *Inside the black box: Raising the standards through classroom assessment.* Retrieved from Phi Delta Kappan: http://blog.discoveryeducation.com/assessment/files/2009/02/blackbox_article.pdf

Black, P., & Wiliam, D. (1998b). Assessment and classroom learning. *Assessment in Education, 5*(1), 7–74.

Bowgren, L., & Sever, K. (2010). *Differentiated professional development in a professional learning community.* Bloomington, IN: Solution Tree Press.

Bybee, R. W., Taylor, J. A., Gardner, A., Van Scotter, P., Powell, J.C., Westbrook, A., & Landes, N. (2006). *The BSCS 5E instructional model: Origins, effectiveness, and applications.* Colorado Springs, CO: BSCS.

Center for Comprehensive School Reform and Improvement. (2007). *Using the classroom walk-through as an instructional leadership strategy.* Retrieved from http://www.centerforcsri.org/index. php?Itemid=5&id=424&option=com_content&task=view

Center of Excellence in Leadership of Learning. (2009). Summary of research on project-based learning. Retrieved from http://cell.uindy.edu/docs/PBL%20research%20summary.pdf

Cordova, D. I., & Lepper, M. R. (1996). Intrinsic motivation and the process of learning: Beneficial effects of contextualization, personalization, and choice. *Journal of Educational Psychology, 88*(4), 715–30.

Costa, A. L., & Garmston, R. J. (1994). *Cognitive coaching: A foundation for Renaissance schools*. Norwood, MA: Chistopher-Gordon.

Council of Chief State School Officers. (2011, April). *Interstate teacher assessment and support consortium (InTASC) model core teaching standards: A resource for state dialogue*. Washington, DC: Author.

David, J. (2008). Classroom walkthroughs. *Educational Leadership, 65*(4), 81–82.

Dochy, F., Segers, M., Van den Bossche, P., & Gijbels, D. (2003). Effects of problem-based learning: A meta-analysis. *Learning and Instruction*, 13, 533–568.

Dotson, J. M. (2001). Cooperative learning structures can increase student achievement. *Kagan Online Magazine*. San Clemente, CA: Kagan Publishing. Retrieved from http://www.kaganonline.com/free_arti cles/research_and_rationale/increase_achievement.php

Downey, C. J., & Frase, L. E. (2001). *Participant's manual for conducting walk-through and reflective feedback to maximize student achievement* (2nd ed.). Huxley, IA: Curriculum Management Services.

Downey, C. J., Steffy, B. E., English, F. W., Frase, L. E., & Poston, W. K., Jr. (2004). *The three-minute classroom walk-through: Changing school supervisory practice one teacher at a time*. Thousand Oaks, CA: Corwin.

Duffy, F. N. (2003). I think, therefore I am resistant to change. *Journal of Staff Development*, (24), 1. Retrieved from http://www.nsdc.org/library/pub lications/jsd/duffy241.cfm

eCybermission, (n.d.). "2002–2011 National Winners." Retrieved July 14, 2013. National Science Teacher's Association Website: http://www.ecy bermission.com/Winners

Elmore, R. (2000). *Building a new structure for school leadership*. Washington, DC: Albert Shanker Institute.

Fuch, L. S., & Fuch, D. (1986). Effects of systematic formative evaluation: A meta-analysis. *Exceptional Children*, 53, 199–208.

Gardner, H. (2011). *Frames of mind: The theory of multiple intelligences* (2nd ed.). New York: Basic Books.

Geier, R., Blumenfeld, P. C., Marx, R. W., Krajcik, J. S., Fishman, B., Soloway, E., & Clay-Chambers, J. (2008). Standardized test outcomes for students engaged in inquiry-based science curricula in the context of urban reform. *Journal of Research in Science Teaching, 45*(8), 922–939.

Gibbs, G. (1992). *Assessing more students*. Oxford, UK: Oxford Brookes University.

Gill, S. (2010). *What gets measured, gets done . . . or not*. Retrieved from http://stephenjgill.typepad.com/performance_improvement_b/2010/02/what-gets-measured-gets-doneor-not.html

Gulek, C. (2003). Preparing for high-stakes testing. *Theory into Practice, 42*(1), 42–50.

Hall, G., & Hord, S. (2000). *Implementing change: Patterns, principles, and potholes*. Boston, MA: Allyn & Bacon.

Hall, G., & Loucks, S. (1979). *Implementing innovations in schools: A concerns-based approach*. Paper presented at the Annual Meeting of the American Educational Research Association, San Francisco, CA.

Hartzler, D. S. (2000). *A meta-analysis of studies conducted on integrated curriculum programs and their effects on student achievement.* (Unpublished dissertation). Indiana University, Bloomington, IN.

Herrington, J., Oliver, R., & Reeves, T. C. (2003). Patterns of engagement in authentic online learning environments. *Australasian Journal of Educational Technology, 19*(1), 59–71.

Hord, S. M., Rutherford, W. L., Huling-Austin, L., Hall, G. E., & Knoll, M. K. (1987). *Taking charge of change.* Alexandria, VA: Association for Supervision and Curriculum Development.

International Center for Research in Education. (n.d.). *Rigor/relevance framework.* Retrieved from http://www.leadered.com/rrr.html

Interstate Teacher Assessment and Support Consortium (a program of CCSSO). (n.d.). *InTASC Model Core Teaching Standards and Learning Progressions for Teachers 1.0.* CreateSpace Independent Publishing Platform, support implementation of the updated InTASC Model Core Teaching Standards and Learning Progressions for Teachers.

Johnson, D. W., & Johnson, R. T. (1999). *Learning together and alone: Cooperative, competitive, and individualistic learning* (5th ed.). Boston, MA: Allyn and Bacon.

Johnson, D. W., Johnson, R. T., & Stanne, M. B. (2000). *Cooperative learning methods: A meta-analysis.* Retrieved from http://www.tablelearning.com/uploads/File/EXHIBIT-B.pdf

Joiner, C. W., Jr. (1987). *Leadership for change.* Cambridge, MA: Ballinger Publishing Company.

Kachur, D. S., Stout, J. A., & Edwards, C. L. (2010). *Classroom walkthroughs to improve teaching and learning.* Larchmont, NY: Eye on Education.

Kahn, S. "Search Khan Academy," on Khan Academy website, retrieved June 10, 2013, https://www.khanacademy.org

Kegerise, S. M. (2007). *Impact of differentiated instructional grouping strategy on fifth grade students' mathematics achievement* (Unpublished dissertation). Widener University, Chester, PA.

Kessner, M. J. (2008). *How does implementation of inquiry-based science instruction in a high-stakes testing environment affect fifth-grade student science achievement?* (Doctoral dissertation). Retrieved from ProQuest Dissertations and Theses. (Accession Order No. AAT 3304567)

Kise, J. A. G. (2006). *Differentiated coaching: A framework for helping teachers change.* Thousand Oaks, CA: Corwin.

Kohl, H. R. (1995). *I won't learn from you—and other thoughts on creative maladjustments.* New York: The New Press.

Kübler-Ross, E., & Kessler, D. (2005). *On grief and grieving: Finding the meaning of grief through the five stages of loss.* New York: Scribner.

Laitsch, D. (2007, June 25). Design-based learning and student achievement. *Research Brief: Translating Education Research into Action, 5*(6), 49–69.

Learning-Theories.com. (n.d.). *Maslow's hierarchy of needs.* Retrieved August 27, 2013, from http://www.learning-theories.com/maslows-hierarchy-of-needs.html

LoTi Connection. (2012). *Atlantic City Board of Education: LoTi Digital Age School Annual Summary.* Carlsbad, CA: Author.

Luster, R. J. (2008). *A quantitative study investigating the effects of whole-class and differentiated instruction on student achievement* (Doctoral dissertation). Retrieved from ProQuest Dissertations and Theses. (Accession Order No. AAT 3320691)

Marzano, R. J. (2007). *The art and science of teaching: A comprehensive framework for effective instruction.* Alexandria, VA: ASCD.

Marzano, R. J. (2012). *Presentation at the New Jersey Association of Federal Program Administrators.* Atlantic City, NJ.

Marzano, R. J., Pickering, D. J., & Pollock, J. E. (2001). *Classroom instruction that works: Research-based strategies for increasing student achievement.* Alexandria, VA: Association for Supervision and Curriculum Development.

Meissner, H. (1999, July 15–19). *Creativity and Mathematics Education.* Summary of International Conference.

Mergendoller, J. R., Maxwell, N., & Bellisimo, Y. (2007). The effectiveness of problem based instruction: A comparative study of instructional methods and student characteristics. *Interdisciplinary Journal of Problem-based Learning, 1*(2), 49–69.

Mississippi Department of Education. (2009). *Webb's depth of knowledge guide: Career and technical education definitions.* Retrieved from http://www.aps.edu/rda/documents/resources/Webbs_DOK_Guide.pdf

Moersch, C. (1995, November). Levels of technology implementation (LoTi): A framework for measuring classroom technology use. *Learning and Leading with Technology,* 40–42.

Moersch, C. (2004). *Experiential-based action model.* Unpublished manuscript.

Moersch, C. (2009). *LoTi math project summary: Year 3 report for Atlantic City Board of Education.* Carlsbad, CA: LoTi Connection.

Moersch, C. (2010). Levels of teaching innovation framework. *Learning & Leading with Technology, 37*(5). Retrieved from www.iste.org (reprinted with permission).

Moersch, C. (2010, February). LoTi turns up the H.E.A.T. *Learning and Leading with Technology, 5*(37), 20–23.

Mueller, J. (2005). The authentic assessment toolbox: Enhancing student learning through online faculty development. *Journal of Online Learning and Teaching, 1*(1).

National Academies. (1996). *National science education standards.* Washington, DC: National Academy Press.

National Association of Secondary School Principals. (n.d.). *NASSP assessment center FAQ.* Retrieved May 13, 2013, from http://www.principals.org/tabid/3788/default.aspx?topic=26776

National Governors Association Center for Best Practices, Common Core State Standards Initiative. (2010). *Common Core State Standards for mathematics.* Retrieved from http://www.corestandards.org

National Governors Association Center for Best Practices, Common Core State Standards Initiative. (2012). *Common Core State Standards initiative: Preparing America's students for college & career.* Retrieved from http://www.corestandards.org

Panitz, T. (2013). *44 benefits of collaborative learning.* Retrieved from http://www.gdrc.org/kmgmt/c-learn/44.html

Papanastasiou, E., Zemblyas, M., & Vrasidas, C. (2003). Can computer use hurt science achievement? *Journal of Science Education and Technology, 12*(3), 325–332.

Partnership for 21st Century Skills. (n.d.). *Framework for 21st century learning.* Retrieved May 10, 2013, from http://www.p21.org/overview

Perez-Prado, A., & Thirunarayanan, M. (2002*).* A qualitative comparison of online and classroom-based sections of a course: Exploring student perspectives. *Education Media International, 39*(2), 195–202.

Pohan, C., & Aguilar, T. (2001, March 20). Measuring educators' beliefs about diversity in personal and professional contexts. *American Educational Research Journal, 38*(1), 159–182.

Preston, J. A. (2008). *Student-centered versus teacher-centered mathematics instruction: A meta-analysis* (Doctoral dissertation). Retrieved from ProQuest, http://gradworks.umi.com/32/89/3289778.html

Randall, D. (n.d.). *The greenhouse effect experiments.* Retrieved July 17, 2013, from http://school.familyeducation.com/outdoor-games/greenhouse-effect/37442.html

Research-based Results. (2008). Retrieved February 1, 2011, from http://www.loticonnection.com/ldas_results.html

Roschelle, J. M., Pea, R. D., Hoadley, C. M., Gordin, D. N., & Means, B. M. (2000). Changing how and what children learn in school with computer-based technologies. *The Future of Children, 10*(2), 76–101.

Salinas, M. F., & Garr, J. (2009a). Effect of learner-centered education on the academic outcomes of minority groups. *Journal of Instructional Psychology, 36*(2), 1–13.

Salinas, M. F., & Garr, J. (2009b). Effects of learner-centered education on the academic outcomes of minority groups. *Journal of Instructional Psychology, 36*(3), 226–237.

Sandy-Hanson, A. E. (2006). *A meta-analysis of the impact of computer technology versus traditional instruction on students in kindergarten through twelfth grade in the United States. A comparison of academic achievement, higher-order thinking skills, motivation, physical outcomes and social skills* (Unpublished dissertation). Howard University, Washington, DC.

Schacter, J. (1999, June). *The impact of education technology on student achievement: What the most current research has to say.* Santa Monica, CA: Milken Exchange on Education Technology.

Schroeder, C. M., Scott, T. P., Tolson, H., Huang, T.-Y., & Lee, Y.-H. (October 30, 2007). A meta-analysis of national research: Effects of teaching strategies on student achievement in science in the United States. *Journal of Research in Science Teaching, 44*(10), 1436–1460.

Senge, P. (n.d.). *Educed: Commentary on education, leadership, and society.* Retrieved May 10, 2013, from http://www.educed.org/?p=233

Shepard, L. A. (2000). The role of classroom assessment in teaching and learning. *Center for the Study of Evaluation (CSE Technical Report # 517).* Los Angeles, CA: University of California.

Siemens, G. (2005, January). Connectivism: A learning theory for the digital age. *International Journal of Instructional Technology & Distance Learning.* Retrieved from http://www.itdl.org/Journal/Jan_05/article01.htm

Slavin, R. E. (1991). Synthesis of research on cooperative learning. *Educational Leadership, 48,* 71–82.

Slavin, R. E. (1995). *Cooperative learning: Theory, research, and practice* (2nd ed.). Boston: Allyn & Bacon.

Slemmer, D. L. (2002). T*he effect of learning styles on student achievement in various hypertext, hypermedia and technology enhanced learning environments: A meta-analysis* (Unpublished dissertation). Boise State University, Boise, ID.

Smith, D. (1996). *A meta-analysis of student outcomes attributable to the teaching of science as inquiry as compared to traditional methodology* (Unpublished dissertation). Temple University, Philadelphia, PA.

Smith, J. (2010). *Types of changes.* Blog: Consulting and Organizational Changes. Retrieved from http://managementhelp.org/blogs/consulting-skills/2010/06/03/types-of-changes/

Stanleigh, M. (2008). *How to successfully manage your change effort.* Retrieved August 27, 2013, from http://www.emeraldinsight.com/learning/management_thinking/articles/pdf/change_effort.pdf?PHPSESSID=brfiatu6ol62lgu08anuhcdhs3

Stiggins, R., & Chappuis, J. (2008, January). Enhancing student learning. *District Administration.* Retrieved from http://www.districtadministration.com/viewarticle.aspx?articleid=1362&p=2#0

Teele, L. (2006). *The impact of integrated study skills and critical thinking on student achievement* (Unpublished dissertation). Capella University, Minneapolis, MN.

Thomas, J. (2000). *A review of research on project-based learning.* Retrieved from www.k12reform.org/foundation/pbl/research/

Tomlinson, C.A. (1999). *How to differentiate instruction in mixed-ability classrooms.* Alexandria, VA: ASCD.

270towin. (n.d.). "Content Display Issues," on 2016 Presidential Election Interactive Map and History of the Electoral College. 270towin, 2004. Retrieved June 10, 2013 from http://www.270towin.com/

U.S. Constitution.net. (n.d.). *U.S. Constitution online,* Retrieved from http://www.usconstitution.net/consttop_stud.html

U.S. Department of Education. (2009). *Race to the top program.* Washington, DC: U.S. Department of Education.

U.S. Environmental Protection Agency. (2013, June 17). *Municipal solid waste.* Retrieved from http://www.epa.gov/epawaste/nonhaz/municipal/index.htm

Wade, E. G. (1994). *A study of the effects of a constructivist-based mathematics problem-solving instructional program on the attitudes, self-confidence, and achievement of post-fifth-grade students.* Retrieved from Dissertations & Theses: Full Text. (Publication No. AAT 9510417)

Walker, A., & Leary, H. (2009). A problem based learning meta analysis: Differences across problem types, implementation types, disciplines, and assessment levels. *Interdisciplinary Journal of Problem-based Learning, 3*(1).

Wallace, M., & Pocklington, K. (2002). *Managing complex educational change: Large-scale reorganisation of schools.* New York, NY: Routledge Falmer.

Wenglinsky, H. (1998). *Does it compute? The relationship between educational technology and student achievement in mathematics.* Princeton, NJ: ETS Policy Information Center.

Westberg, K. L., & Archambault, F. X. (2004). *A multi-site case study of successful classroom practices for high ability students in differentiation for gifted and talented students.* Thousand Oaks, CA: Corwin and National Association for Gifted Children.

Wiggins, G. (2012, January). *What works in education–Hattie's list of the greatest effects and why it matters* [Web blog post]. Retrieved from http:// grantwiggins.wordpress.com/2012/01/07/what-works-in-education-hatties-list-of-the-greatest-effects-and-why-it-matters/

Wikipedia. (n.d.). Image of Maslow's Hierarchy of Needs. Retrieved August 23, 2013, from https://en.wikipedia.org/wiki/File%3AMaslow%27s_ Hierarchy_of_Needs.svg

Wininger, R. S. (2005). Using your tests to teach: Formative summative assessment. *Teaching Psychology, 32*(2), 164–166.

Index